When FOOTBALL Was FOOTBALL

RANGERS

© Haynes Publishing, 2010

First published in 2010

A catalogue record for this book is available from the British Library

ISBN: 978-0-857330-36-9

Published by Haynes Publishing, Sparkford, Yeovil,
Somerset BA22 7JJ, UK
Tel: 01963 442030 Fax: 01963 440001
Int. tel: +44 1963 442030 Int. fax: +44 1963 440001
E-mail: sales@haynes.co.uk
Website: www.haynes.co.uk

Haynes North America Inc., 861 Lawrence Drive,
Newbury Park, California 91320, USA

All images © Mirrorpix

Creative Director: Kevin Gardner
Designed for Haynes by BrainWave

Printed and bound in the US

When
FOOTBALL *Was*
FOOTBALL

RANGERS

A Nostalgic Look at a Century of the Club

Ronnie Esplin

Contents

Introduction

Scottish football and the Scottish newspaper industry are inextricably linked. Long before the amateurs of Queen's Park helped popularize the game in Scotland in the second half of the 19th century, newspapers were part of everyday life.

The Press, though, helped football become the national sport while simultaneously benefiting from the fans' voracious appetite for news on their team and their favourite players.

Over the years the *Daily Record* and its sister papers have provided an invaluable service for the predominantly working-class football supporter and amid blanket coverage of the Scottish game they have chronicled the highs and lows of Rangers Football Club.

The photographs in this book give fresh life to great games and famous players associated with the Ibrox club. The glories and the tragedies are captured; the Hampden riots of 1909 and 1980, the Iron Curtain side of the 50s, the Ibrox disaster in 1971, victory in Europe a year later and the nine-in-a-row title winning teams of 1989-1997.

Legendary Rangers figures such as Bill Struth, Willie Waddell, Jim Baxter, John Greig, Jock Wallace, Ally McCoist and Walter Smith are featured as are numerous other characters who have played their part over the years in bringing almost constant success to the Govan club.

During troubled times for the game in Scotland and worries over the future of Rangers, these pictures remind fans of the club's growth over more than a century, since that day in 1872 when four teenagers thought to get themselves involved in the craze of the time, association football.

The Gallant Pioneers
1872-1919

The Rangers team that played in the 1877 Scottish Cup final against the then mighty Vale of Leven. Back row (left to right): George Gillespie, William McNeil, James Watt, Sam Ricketts. Middle row (left to right): William Dunlop, David Hill, Tom Vallance, Peter Campbell, Moses McNeil. Front row (left to right): James Watson, Sandy Marshall. Rangers had reached the final just five years after the club's formation. Two of the founders, Moses McNeil and Peter Campbell, are in the line-up, as is one of the club's most influential personalities in its early days, Tom Vallance, who wears a different badge from his team-mates, the lion rampant, to signify two international appearances for Scotland that season. After two 1-1 draws, Rangers lost the second replay 3-2, but their performances against Vale brought them great prestige.

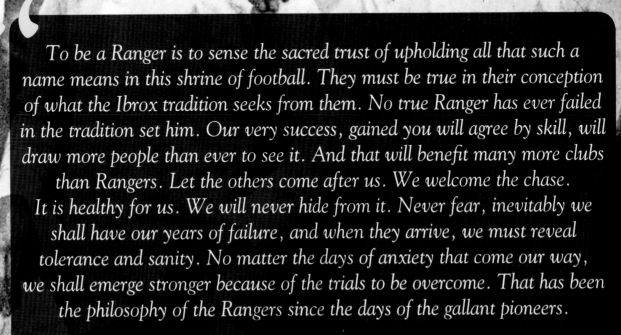

"
To be a Ranger is to sense the sacred trust of upholding all that such a name means in this shrine of football. They must be true in their conception of what the Ibrox tradition seeks from them. No true Ranger has ever failed in the tradition set him. Our very success, gained you will agree by skill, will draw more people than ever to see it. And that will benefit many more clubs than Rangers. Let the others come after us. We welcome the chase. It is healthy for us. We will never hide from it. Never fear, inevitably we shall have our years of failure, and when they arrive, we must reveal tolerance and sanity. No matter the days of anxiety that come our way, we shall emerge stronger because of the trials to be overcome. That has been the philosophy of the Rangers since the days of the gallant pioneers.

Bill Struth, long-time Rangers manager
"

1872 Brothers Peter and Moses McNeil, William McBeath and Peter Campbell – all teenagers – decide to form a football team. Moses McNeil suggested the name Rangers after seeing the name in a book about English Rugby. Rangers play their first two games that season, drawing 0-0 with Callendar and beating a team called Clyde 11-0 (not the present Clyde). 1877 Rangers lose in the Scottish Cup final to Vale of Leven after the second replay and also lose to the same team in the final two years later (this time declining to take part in a replay following an unsuccessful protest). 1888 Celtic Football Club are formed in the east end of Glasgow and beat Rangers 5-2 in a friendly in their first meeting. 1890 The Scottish league is formed and Rangers finish joint-top with Dumbarton, and after a play-off match finish 2-2: the title is shared for the first and only time. 1894 At the third time of asking Rangers taste their first Scottish Cup final success with a 3-1 win over Celtic. 1899 Rangers become a limited company and match secretary William Wilton is appointed as the club's first manager. They take the title that season in record style, winning every one of their 18 league matches. 1914 Bill Struth joins Rangers as trainer from Clyde.

Rangers team, which beat Celtic to win the Scottish Cup for the first time in 1894. Also pictured is the Glasgow Cup.

LEFT: Rangers team of 1896/97. The Scottish Cup, the Glasgow Cup and the Glasgow Merchant's charity cup were captured that season.

Old Firm United

Rangers and Celtic are renowned for their historic and often bitter rivalry, but it was not always thus. It is believed that the term 'Old Firm' originated during the early year of the 20th century and was in part meant as a jibe at the financial benefits both clubs enjoyed from their frequent meetings. There had been a history of draws between the clubs in the Glasgow Cup. Could these games have been rigged to make more money from replays? Certainly that appeared to be the collective view of some Rangers and Celtic fans after the 1909 Scottish Cup final replay at Hampden ended 1-1. It was incorrectly thought that there would be extra time. When it became clear there would be a second replay, fans from both teams stormed the pitch and, among various misdemeanours, set fire to turnstiles and fought with the fire brigade. The Cup was withheld that season.

Hampden burns after Old Firm fans riot.

Rangers and Celtic players linger on the pitch after the 1-1 draw in the Scottish Cup final, unsure of what was to happen next. The supporters were soon to invade.

Growing with Glory
1920-1954

Rangers v Hamilton Academical in the 1935 Scottish Cup final at Hampden. Accies keeper Jimmy Morgan saves from Bobby Main but the Ibrox club, watched by a crowd of 87,740, captured the trophy for the ninth time with a 2-1 win.

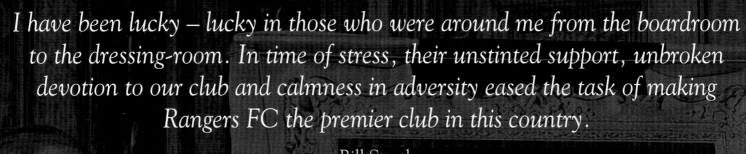

I have been lucky – lucky in those who were around me from the boardroom to the dressing-room. In time of stress, their unstinted support, unbroken devotion to our club and calmness in adversity eased the task of making Rangers FC the premier club in this country.

Bill Struth

Newspaper picture of Rangers' first manager, William Wilton, who died in a tragic boating accident off Gourock in 1920, a day after the league title was won.

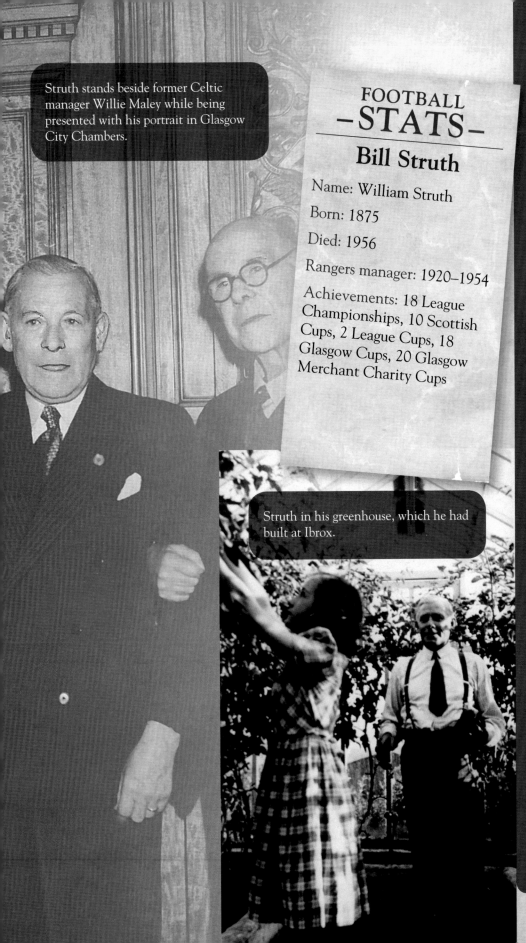

Struth stands beside former Celtic manager Willie Maley while being presented with his portrait in Glasgow City Chambers.

FOOTBALL
–STATS–
Bill Struth

Name: William Struth

Born: 1875

Died: 1956

Rangers manager: 1920–1954

Achievements: 18 League Championships, 10 Scottish Cups, 2 League Cups, 18 Glasgow Cups, 20 Glasgow Merchant Charity Cups

Struth in his greenhouse, which he had built at Ibrox.

–LEGENDS–

Bill Struth

Bill Struth's incredible record of success as Rangers manager during a remarkable 34 years in the hot seat is unarguable. He took over the club in 1920 when Rangers' first boss, William Wilton, who had recruited him as a trainer in 1914, died in a boating accident.

However, all the cups and trophies he gathered over three decades and more almost pale into significance when his legacy at the Ibrox club is assessed. With Struth it was all about standards. The former stonemason carved deep into the Ibrox psyche not only the need to be the best but to look the best and act the best.

Struth reigned over some of the greatest figures in the club's history, a lineage which includes a succession of Light Blues heroes such as David Meiklejohn, Alan Morton, Willie Waddell, Willie Thornton, Jock Shaw, George Young and Willie Woodburn. And they all knew Struth was the boss.

A traditional authoritarian figure of his time, he believed in respect and manners. The Rangers players had to wear a collar and tie to training. They travelled first class with the club but were expected to pay for the best seats when they went to the cinema in their leisure time. Rangers had to be the best.

Struth became a director of Rangers in 1947 and was appointed vice-chairman on his retirement as manager in the summer of 1954. He died two years later, aged 81. Struth's imposing portrait (featured left) now hangs in the famous Ibrox trophy room.

The Scottish Cup returns to Ibrox.

RIGHT: One youngster tries to sneak in to Hampden for the 1928 Scottish Cup final between Rangers and Celtic while his two pals wait to follow.

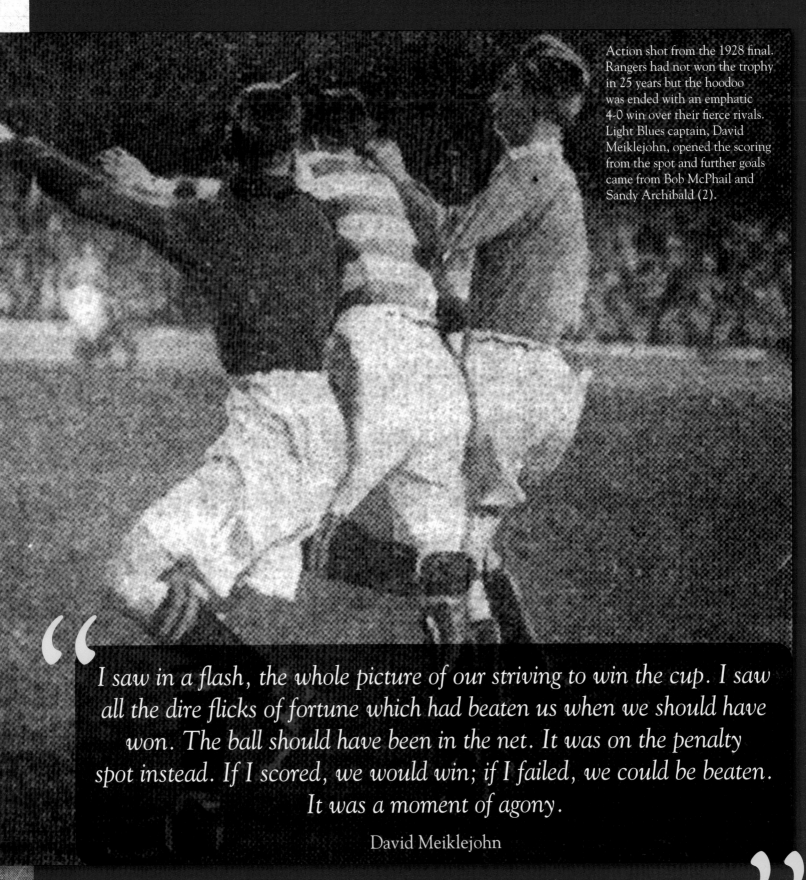

Action shot from the 1928 final. Rangers had not won the trophy in 25 years but the hoodoo was ended with an emphatic 4-0 win over their fierce rivals. Light Blues captain, David Meiklejohn, opened the scoring from the spot and further goals came from Bob McPhail and Sandy Archibald (2).

I saw in a flash, the whole picture of our striving to win the cup. I saw all the dire flicks of fortune which had beaten us when we should have won. The ball should have been in the net. It was on the penalty spot instead. If I scored, we would win; if I failed, we could be beaten. It was a moment of agony.

David Meiklejohn

–LEGENDS–

Alan Morton

Every visitor who enters through the front door at Ibrox will see the famous portrait of Alan Morton at the top of the equally famous marble staircase.

Morton was Bill Struth's first signing for the club in 1920, and that his picture takes pride of place at the stadium is testament to his legacy. The diminutive winger stood at only 5ft 4ins but he terrorized defences up and down Scotland, and in his 13 years as a player in Govan the club won 10 First Division championships and two Scottish Cups.

The former Queen's Park player displayed his talents in the dark blue of Scotland as well as the light blue of Rangers. Of his 31 caps for Scotland, 11 were earned against the "Auld Enemy" and he earned his nickname of the "Wee Blue Devil" after his performance against England in 1928, when the "Wembley Wizards" beat the hosts 5-1. He was director of Rangers from 1933 until his death in 1971.

Morton prepares to take on Celtic in 1945.

FOOTBALL –STATS–

Alan Morton

Name: Alan Lauder Morton

Born: 1893

Died: 1971

Playing career: Rangers 1920–1933

Appearances: 495

Goals: 115

"

The wee man was simply a magician.

Bob McPhail

"

ABOVE: Moscow Dynamo visited Britain for a series of friendlies in 1945 and were unbeaten against Chelsea, Arsenal and Cardiff before they travelled to Glasgow in November to take on Rangers. The game was played in the afternoon but still attracted a massive crowd of 95,000 who watched a 2-2 draw, with the Russians playing for a spell with 12 men, until it was pointed out to the referee. Rangers skipper George Young would later joke that he had met every schoolboy who had played truant to watch a unique match which is now part of Ibrox folklore.

LEFT: Rangers line-up in 1947. In traditional fashion, team pictures were taken before games.

ABOVE: Stranraer v Rangers, January 1948. A packed Stair Park sees home keeper Park defy a Rangers attack in this Scottish Cup tie, but a Willie Thornton goal gave the visitors (playing in hoops) a 1-0 win.

LEFT: Street scene at Ibrox in 1948. This would have been the view of the stadium fans would see after turning off Paisley Road West and into Edmiston Drive.

American actor and comedian Danny Kaye walks out on the Hampden pitch before the 1950 Charity Cup final between Rangers and Celtic which the Parkhead side won 3-2.

1950. Rangers keeper Bobby Brown watches the ball slide past the post as Hibs press at Ibrox. The Edinburgh side were Rangers main rivals at that time and beat the Light Blues to the title in 1951 and 1952.

—LEGENDS—

George Young

George Young was a colossus of a captain for Rangers and Scotland and an integral part of the Ibrox club's famous "Iron Curtain" defence of the 1940s and 1950s: Bobby Brown, George Young, Jock Shaw, Ian McColl, Willie Woodburn and Sammy Cox.

Young won what was then a record 53 caps for Scotland – 48 of them as skipper – and played in 34 consecutive internationals. Standing 6ft 2ins and weighing around 15 stone, Young dominated in every way. Old-time Rangers fans of that era would often argue about who was the better player, Young or his contemporary, Willie Woodburn. It is accepted that Young had the edge in that although he was a natural centre-half he was good enough to be switched to right-back to allow Woodburn to play at the heart of the Gers defence.

Young won the first of his six Championships in the 1946/7 season. He also collected one of his two League Cups as Rangers became the first winners of the new trophy with a 4-0 victory over Aberdeen in the final. "Corky" also won four Scottish Cup medals and later managed Third Lanark for three years.

April 1953. Scottish Cup final at Hampden. Young is held aloft by team-mates after Rangers had beaten Aberdeen 1-0.

"He was like a giant octopus. You would beat him seven times in one move, and thought you were past him, then that eighth leg would come out to reclaim the ball.

England and Preston star Tom Finney

Scotland v Yugoslavia, Hampden, November 1956. Captain Young shakes hands with Dejan Stanković.

BELOW: Young looks back at his achievements, circa 1960s.

Training 1950s Style

LEFT: July 1953 and Rangers skipper George Young is pushed on the Ibrox lawnmower by his team-mates, among whom is Jock "Tiger" Shaw and Willie Woodburn.

BELOW: Lapping the park was the main form of pre-season training, and indeed day-to-day training, for footballers in the 1950s. Despite it being July the players are wearing heavy polo-necked tops and jogging trousers.

Rangers blazer badge inscribed with 1873. For many years there was some confusion about the date of the club's formation and it celebrated its centenary in 1973. It is only in recent years and after some research by football historians and journalists that the club has accepted it was formed in 1872.

Rangers players and their wives arrive back from the 1954 tour of North America. The players are smartly dressed with club blazers and ties despite the length of journey – it took a week to get there and a week to get back! Rangers played nine games between 16th May and 6th June, including three against Chelsea. The Ibrox side won seven matches, lost one and drew one against the Londoners. As can be seen, smoking was common in post-war Britain, even among footballers.

A new era. Scot Symon stands with his Rangers side in August 1954 as they pose for pictures ahead of the new season.

Symon, a former Ibrox player, enjoyed success as a manager at East Fife and Preston North End before he took over from Struth to become Rangers' third manager. He would enjoy plenty of success for the rest of the decade and in the early 1960s, but unfortunately, for those of a light blue persuasion, the tables would turn...

New Challenges
1955-1971

Rangers were at the forefront when European club football was initiated in the 1950s. The Ibrox club entered the European Cup in the 1955/6 season when it was a tournament for champions only, but after getting a bye in the first round they lost to French club OGC Nice in a play-off, curiously, in Paris, after both sides had won their home legs 2-1. The following season Rangers were back in the European Cup after winning the Scottish League title again and were paired with another French club, St Etienne. After a 3-1 win at Ibrox, the Light Blues lost 2-1 in the second leg in France to go through to the second round where they would meet AC Milan. However, the Italian giants handed out a tough lesson to Scot Symon's men, winning 4-1 in Govan before completing the job with a 2-0 win in Italy. The Light Blues fans would get used to those continental highs and lows in the coming years.

Rangers keeper Niven is beaten by a shot from St Etienne winger Njo Lea with Bobby Shearer looking on and Ian McColl in the background, but the ball runs wide. The home side are wearing their change strip of white shirt with blue and red band, and fetching satin blue shorts.

1956–7 Rangers enter the European Cup for the first time but go out to French team Nice. 1960 Jim Baxter signs from Raith Rovers for £17,500. Rangers reach the semi-finals of the European Cup, losing eventually to German club Eintracht Frankfurt by a record aggregate 12-4 for a Scottish team. 1961 Rangers become the first British team to reach a European final when they play Fiorentina in the Cup Winners' Cup final but lose 4-1 on aggregate. 1962 The Ibrox club go on a groundbreaking tour of Moscow where future skipper and manager John Greig comes to the fore. 1966 Kai Johansen scores the winner in the replayed Old Firm Scottish Cup final at Hampden. 1967 Rangers suffer a shock Scottish Cup defeat by Berwick Rangers but reach the final of the Cup Winners' Cup where they lose 1-0 to Bayern Munich in Nuremberg. Scot Symon is dismissed and Davie White is installed as Rangers' fourth manager. 1969 White is sacked after European exit to Gornik; club legend Willie Waddell is appointed as manager. 1971 Ibrox disaster; 66 people die in a crush on stairway 13 following a drawn Old Firm game.

BELOW: The return game in France sees Rangers, back to wearing their v-necked blue shirts and blue shorts, under pressure.

RIGHT: November 1957 and the AC Milan squad assemble at Ibrox for a training session the night before the first leg of the European Cup second-round tie.

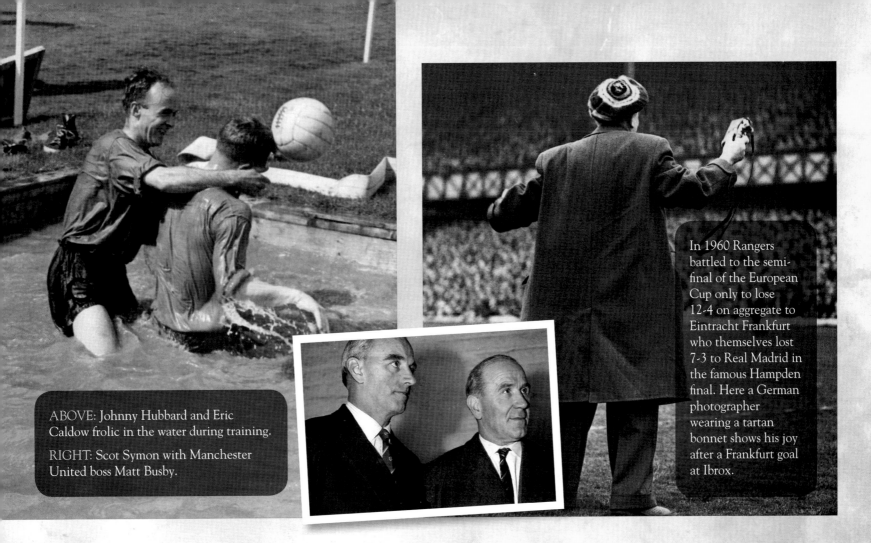

ABOVE: Johnny Hubbard and Eric Caldow frolic in the water during training.

RIGHT: Scot Symon with Manchester United boss Matt Busby.

In 1960 Rangers battled to the semi-final of the European Cup only to lose 12-4 on aggregate to Eintracht Frankfurt who themselves lost 7-3 to Real Madrid in the famous Hampden final. Here a German photographer wearing a tartan bonnet shows his joy after a Frankfurt goal at Ibrox.

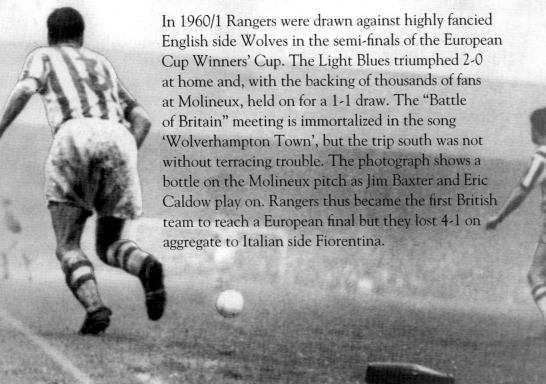

In 1960/1 Rangers were drawn against highly fancied English side Wolves in the semi-finals of the European Cup Winners' Cup. The Light Blues triumphed 2-0 at home and, with the backing of thousands of fans at Molineux, held on for a 1-1 draw. The "Battle of Britain" meeting is immortalized in the song 'Wolverhampton Town', but the trip south was not without terracing trouble. The photograph shows a bottle on the Molineux pitch as Jim Baxter and Eric Caldow play on. Rangers thus became the first British team to reach a European final but they lost 4-1 on aggregate to Italian side Fiorentina.

"It was down at Wolverhampton not so very long ago
And to our local Englishmen we did put on a show
Ten thousand strong we marched along to hear the famous noise
For we're the lads, the lads that follow Rangers.

So on Rangers on, victory is near,
From the terraces you will hear the cry
So come along with Rangers, you'll know us by our noise
For we're the lads, the lads that follow Rangers"

One version of a Rangers song that stemmed from the game against Wolverhampton.

To Russia with Love

In the summer of 1962, during the Cold War, Rangers flew to the Soviet Union for a three-match tour. The Light Blues returned unbeaten after a 3-1 victory over Lokomotiv Moscow, a 1-0 triumph over Dynamo Tbilisi of Georgia and a 1-1 draw with Dynamo Kiev. At a time when the Soviet Union was still shrouded in mystery, the tour caught the imagination of the Scottish public. Thousands of Rangers fans turned up at Renfrew airport (now called Glasgow airport) to welcome the team back and caused some chaos when they streamed on to the runway after the plane landed.

LEFT & BELOW: The Rangers plane mobbed by thousands of supporters.

Rangers squad enjoying some sightseeing in Moscow. Included in the picture is Willie Henderson, Ralph Brand, Ian McMillan, Eric Caldow, Davie Provan and Davie Wilson.

Another Battle of Britain

In the second round of the 1962/3 European Cup Winners' Cup, Rangers were drawn to play English double winners Tottenham Hotspur. In this "Battle of Britain" it was the English side, fresh from winning the double, who came out on top. The Light Blues lost 5-2 in London and 3-2 at Ibrox.

Rangers players train at White Hart Lane before the first leg.

The Ibrox players enjoy a meal the night before the game in London.

Scot Symon with Spurs boss Bill Nicholson.

ABOVE: Bobby Shearer under pressure from Cliff Jones as Ronnie McKinnon looks on.

LEFT: Rangers fans outside White Hart Lane, one playing the bagpipes.

RIGHT: Bobby Shearer exchanges pennants with Danny Blanchflower before the second leg at Ibrox.

Rangers played all-conquering Real Madrid in the first round of the 1963/4 European Cup. It was another tough European lesson learned by the Govan club. After losing 1-0 at Ibrox to a late Puskás goal, Rangers travelled to Madrid with a weakened team for the return game and were crushed 6-0.

BELOW: Madrid's famous striker, Francisco Gento, steps down from the team bus outside Ibrox to be met by enthusiastic autograph hunters.

Real Madrid players ignore the sign as they train at Ibrox the night before the first leg.

Singing Sixties

ABOVE: March 1963 and Rangers players including Jim Baxter, Davie Wilson, Ronnie McKinnon and Bobby Shearer are in the studio recording a Rangers song.

LEFT: May 1963 and Rangers players get in tune with a song for the Freedom from Hunger Campaign. The front three are Davie Wilson, Bobby Shearer and Willie Henderson, with Norrie Martin, Ronnie McKinnon and Davie Provan behind.

ABOVE: No corporate boxes or prawn sandwiches for the Rangers WAGS of the 1960s as they watch their men at work.

LEFT: Glasgow-born pop star Lulu sits on Alec Willoughby's knee, with Willie Henderson at the side and Craig Watson and Ronnie McKinnon behind.

Quiz Ball was a successful television sports quiz programme of the 1960s and early 1970s. Here John Greig, composer Bill Martin, Jim Baxter and Dave Smith stand at the side of the Celtic team.

WILLIE WALLACE

JIM CRAIG

JOHN CAIRNEY

CELTIC

World Champion boxer Sugar Ray Robinson is introduced to the crowd at Ibrox during the interval in the match against Dunfermline in 1964.

BILLY McN

Cup Glory

Bobby Shearer is held aloft by his team-mates at Hampden after
Rangers had beaten Dundee 3-1 in the 1964 Scottish Cup final.
Davie Wilson is crouching, wearing the bowler hat.

Bobby Shearer leads his Rangers side on the lap of honour.

–LEGENDS–

Jim Baxter

There are many Ibrox fans of a certain generation who believe "Slim Jim" Baxter was the greatest Ranger of them all, and there is no doubt that the talented midfielder with the swagger and classy left foot lit up the Sixties for club and country.

Signed from Raith Rovers in 1960 for a then record fee of £17,500, the Fifer had an incredible record against Celtic which he cherished. In 18 games against the Parkhead men – 10 League, five League Cup and three Scottish Cup – he lost only twice.

Baxter broke his leg during a 2-0 European Cup tie away victory to Rapid Vienna in December 1964 and many supporters believe that with that accident disappeared a genuine chance for Rangers to become the first British club to win the trophy.

He was also the scourge of England and his keepy-up against the then World Champions at Wembley in 1967 is an enduring image for all football fans – even though he was no longer at Ibrox at that stage in his career.

In 1965 he was transferred to Sunderland for £72,500, then followed a move to Nottingham Forest for £100,000 two years later – but by then his off-field activities were taking their toll. His return to Rangers in 1969 was unsuccessful and in December 1970 he retired from the game at the age of 31. Baxter lost his fight with cancer at the age of 61 on 14th April 2001.

Baxter holds aloft the League Cup to an almost empty Celtic end of Hampden following the 2-1 win in October 1964.

" *Baxter was Rangers' greatest-ever player and would have been a great player in any era.*

Sir Alex Ferguson

> *The wives of Celtic fans used to send me letters thanking me for sending their husbands home early.*
>
> Jim Baxter

ABOVE: Baxter on National Service, which caused him to miss the tour of Russia in 1962.

LEFT: Baxter plays the Pied Piper with admiring youngsters as he strolls away from Ibrox.

BELOW: Baxter, in his second spell at Rangers, takes the acclaim of the crowd at Ibrox with a bottle of champagne in hand.

FOOTBALL -STATS-

Jim Baxter

Name: James Curran Baxter

Born: 1939

Died: 2001

Playing career: Rangers 1960–65, 69–70

Appearances: 254

Goals: 24

The Kai Johansen final

Kai Johansen entered Rangers folklore when he scored the winner against Celtic in the replayed 1966 Scottish Cup final at Hampden. The Danish defender was the first foreigner to score in a Scottish Cup final and it was his first goal for the club.

Back row, left to right: Watson, Miller, Johansen, Ritchie, McKinnon, Provan, Greig:

Front row, left to right: Henderson, Willoughby, Sorensen, Forrest, McLean, Johnston and Wilson.

John Greig and Celtic skipper Billy McNeill at the coin toss with legendary referee Tiny Wharton before the first game on the Saturday, which ended goalless.

Rangers fans at the final.

Ronnie Simpson saves from Jim Forrest, with Billy McNeill in attendance. The picture captures magnificently the sheer size of Hampden and the crowds that would regularly attend big games.

ABOVE: Johansen (out of picture) lights up the gloom of the Hampden darkness in the evening replay with his drive which leaves Celtic keeper Ronnie Simpson flailing; Tommy Gemmell, Billy McNeill and George McLean are watching.

RIGHT: "King Kai" celebrates. Celtic midfielder Bertie Auld, who is not too happy, is in the foreground.

RIGHT: Scot Symon and his wife with the cup.

BELOW: Rangers players returned to the St Enoch Hotel in Glasgow city centre and celebrated the Cup win with the fans.

ABOVE: The Russian connection with Rangers continues. On 11th February 1967 Aleksei Kosygin, a senior Soviet statesman (Chairman of the Council of Ministers from 1964–1980), meets Alec Willoughby before a game against Kilmarnock at Rugby Park.

LEFT: May 1967 and Rangers fans are in a cheerful mood.

Wallace clutches from McLean and Forrest.

After the Pride comes the Fall

After winning the Scottish Cup in 1966, Rangers suffered the biggest shock in the club's history in the first round the following season when they lost 1-0 away to lowly Berwick Rangers. Ironically, in goal for Berwick was Jock Wallace, who would in time become a Rangers legend as boss of his boyhood heroes. The defeat signalled the end of Ibrox strikers Jim Forrest and George McLean, both of whom were effectively blamed for the defeat, dropped and sold within weeks.

> *Some of these players will never wear the jersey again.*
>
> Statement from Rangers after the game

Rangers keeper Norrie Martin lies on the ground as joyful Berwick players celebrate Sammy Reid's famous goal.

Fans of both sides invade the park after the game as the Berwick players try to get off.

New Era

In November 1967, with Rangers top of the league and unbeaten, Scot Symon departed under controversial circumstances and was replaced by Davie White. The previous season Rangers had recovered from the Berwick calamity to reach the final of the European Cup Winners' Cup, where they had lost 1-0 to Bayern Munich after extra time in Nuremberg. Despite being at Rangers since 1954, Symon was not afforded the courtesy of a face-to-face meeting with any of the Ibrox powerbrokers; instead, he was informed of his fate by an associate of the Board.

New Rangers assistant Davie White is shown Ibrox by Scot Symon.

In April 1968 large screens were erected at Ibrox to show the second leg of the Inter-Cities Fairs Cup tie between Leeds United and Rangers at Elland Road. The first game in Glasgow was goalless, but the Yorkshire side won 2-0 in the return leg.

Rangers players in training. Note Alex Ferguson wearing the No. 9 kit. Just as Forrest and McLean were made scapegoats for the Berwick defeat, Ferguson was blamed for allowing Billy McNeill to score the opening goal for Celtic in the 1969 Scottish Cup final, which the Parkhead side won 4-0.

1969 Scottish Cup final and Norrie Martin saves from Billy McNeill with Ronnie McKinnon and Alex Ferguson in close attendance and Stevie Chalmers ready to pounce.

—LEGENDS—

Johnstone rounding Kilmarnock keeper Jim Stewart at Rugby Park in 1974.

Derek Johnstone

Johnstone became an instant legend at the tender age of 16 years (and 355 days) when he scored the only goal of the game in the 1970 League Cup final against Celtic at Hampden. Five months previously he had still been at school. It was the first trophy the Ibrox club had won since 1966 and ended a five-year run of League Cup successes by their bitter rivals.

The big Dundonian proved to be as adept at centre-half as centre-forward and played in defence when Rangers won the European Cup Winners' Cup final against Moscow Dynamo in Barcelona two years later.

But it was as a striker he made his name, winning trebles at Ibrox in 1975/6 and 1977/8 and earning a place in the Scotland squad for the 1978 World Cup in Argentina. Why he was kept on the bench for all three games by Ally MacLeod remains one of Scottish football's great mysteries. "DJ" left Ibrox in 1983 to play for Chelsea, but returned in 1985 before retiring a year later.

> *It was at 3.41pm on Saturday, 24ᵗʰ October 1970 when my life changed.*
>
> Derek Johnstone

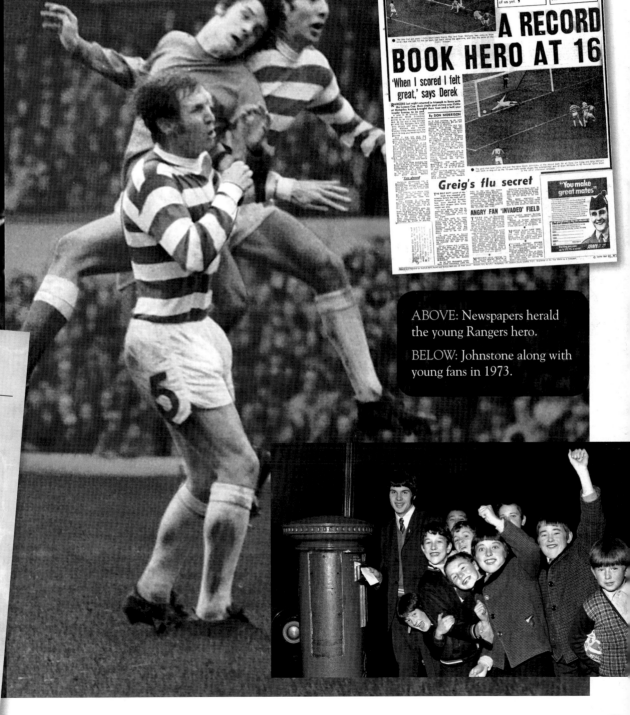

> *Derek Johnstone was my hero.*
>
> Ally McCoist

Johnstone climbs above Billy McNeill and Jim Craig to score his famous winner.

ABOVE: Newspapers herald the young Rangers hero.

BELOW: Johnstone along with young fans in 1973.

FOOTBALL –STATS–

Derek Johnstone

Name: Derek Joseph Johnstone

Born: 1953

Playing career: Rangers 1970–83, 85–6

Appearances: 546

Goals: 210

Ibrox Disaster

On 2nd January 1971, 66 people died and over 200 were injured in the Ibrox disaster which followed an Old Firm game. After Celtic took the lead in the 89th minute through Jimmy Johnstone many Rangers supporters began to leave the stadium. However, in the last seconds of stoppage time, Colin Stein scored an equalizer. Initially it was believed that the crush on the infamous stairway 13 was due to fans turning back on hearing the roars, but this was later proved to be untrue: it was the sheer volume of people departing down the stairs that had led to mayhem and panic.

Sadly, it was not the first Ibrox disaster. In 1902 a section of the old wooden terracing collapsed under the weight of too many spectators during a Scotland v England game. A total of 25 people died and 587 were injured. The match was replayed at Villa Park a month later, finishing 2-2. On 16th September 1961 two people were killed in a crush on the stairway, and although improvements had been made, the 1971 disaster led in time to the revamp of the stadium, led by Willie Waddell, then general manager. The stadium was eventually converted to an all-seater stadium, and was subsequently awarded UEFA five-star status. The statue of John Greig outside the main stand commemorates those killed in the tragedy.

RIGHT: Celtic manager Jock Stein and Willie Waddell help lift a victim on to a stretcher.

SUNDAY MAIL

108 injured, and boys are among the dead

3245 JANUARY 3, 1971

66 KILLED IN IBROX DISASTER

SIXTY-SIX spectators were killed and another 108 injured—three critically in Britain's biggest-ever football tragedy at Ibrox Park, Glasgow, yesterday.

It came at the end of a trouble-free match between Rangers and Celtic watched by 80,000 spectators.

Just before the end of the match, Rangers fans on their way out heard the roar of the crowd as Rangers scored a last seconds equalising goal.

Many tried to get back up the steps to the ground, but were engulfed by hundreds of other fans swarming down after the final whistle.

Crush barriers on the stairway were broken by the crowds . . . and fans fell on top of one another.

Lord Provost Sir Donald Liddle, weeping at a Press conference, said: "It is quite clear a great many died of suffocation."

The Chief Constable, Sir James Robertson, said it was clear that barricades had burst and fans had piled on top of each other.

Fans help injured

Ambulances, fire engines and police cars were rushed to the stadium. Some had difficulty in reaching the scene because home-going crowds from the match were unaware of the tragedy.

As well as the official figures, many more were treated on the spot by first aid men and doctors from among the spectators.

Police appealed to spectators who had escaped disaster to help in carrying stretchers.

Many friends, still wearing their club colours, helped carry dead and injured to the pavilion.

Club officials worked in their shirt sleeves, helping to injured spectators.

The first bodies were extricated and brought

Continued on Page Two

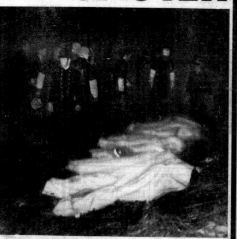

Shrouded bodies lie in rows on the Ibrox turf.

POLICE NAME THE DEAD—SEE BACK PAGE

PICTURES PAGES 3, 4, 5, 7, 9

"

The disaster will never leave me. Never a day goes by that it doesn't go through my mind. I still get letters from guys who have never been back to Ibrox for a game since that day.

John Greig

"

ABOVE: The emergency services working hard at Ibrox as bodies are laid along the goal line.

LEFT: Staircase 13 at the "Rangers end" of Ibrox where the tragedy occurred. The reinforced fencing down the sides prevented fans spilling out on to the grassy banks.

RIGHT: Willie Waddell effectively took control of the club in the wake of the disaster . He ensured there was a Rangers representative at every funeral and players also visited the injured in hospital. Here, Willie Mathieson and John Greig are at the city's Victoria Hospital.

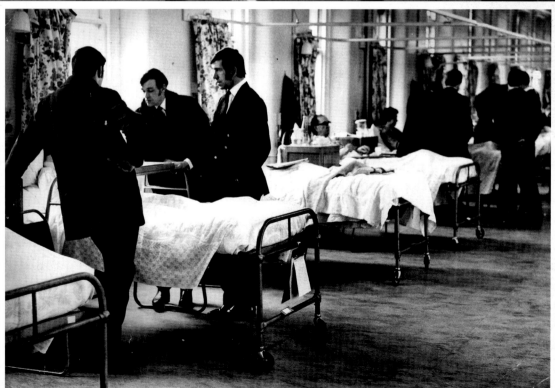

1972: European Success
AT LAST

Rangers enjoyed a measure of European success in the Sixties but it was 1972 before they eventually captured a European trophy. The Govan club, still recovering from the Ibrox disaster the previous year, went on an impressive run in the Cup Winners' Cup, beating Rennes, Sporting Lisbon, Torino and Bayern Munich before overcoming Moscow Dynamo 3-2 in a dramatic and eventful final at the Nou Camp.

Previous manager Scot Symon had guided the club to two European finals. In 1961 Rangers lost the first Cup Winners' Cup final to Fiorentina 4-1 on aggregate and in the final of the same tournament in 1967, they succumbed 1-0 to Bayern Munich after extra time in Nuremberg.

However, in Spain it was to be third time lucky for the Ibrox club. Around 25,000 fans travelled to the home of Barcelona, many leaving Scotland for the first time, to see the Light Blues race in to a three-goal lead with strikes from Colin Stein and Willie Johnston (2) then hang on in dogged fashion until the final whistle.

Rangers v Fiorentina, May 1961, Billy Ritchie saves from Kurt Hamrin. In an ill-tempered game in front of 80,000 fans at Ibrox in the first leg, Eric Caldow missed a first-half penalty as the Italians won 2-0 to make the return game in Florence a formality. Despite Alex Scott scoring for Rangers the Italians won 2-1 to take the trophy.

Referee Erich Steiner is surrounded by Fiorentina players and is about to be accosted by the Italian club's assistant coach, Chiapella, after Rangers were awarded a penalty.

ABOVE: Caldow puts his penalty kick wide of the post with goalkeeper Albertosi beaten.

LEFT: Fiorentina's Luigi Milan is congratulated by team-mates after scoring the second goal past Rangers' goalkeeper Ritchie.

Auf Wiedersehen Rangers

RIGHT: John Greig and Davie Provan are settled in by an air hostess as Rangers fly to Nuremberg for the 1967 European Cup Winners' Cup final against Bayern Munich.

RIGHT: Wilson, Greig, Henderson and Ritchie going through their paces in the empty stadium before the Nuremberg final. With the match being played in Germany, Bayern would win the vast majority of the support in the 65,000 crowd. Bizarrely, Rangers chairman John Lawrence highlighted the shortcomings of the Ibrox side the day before the game, which did little to boost confidence.

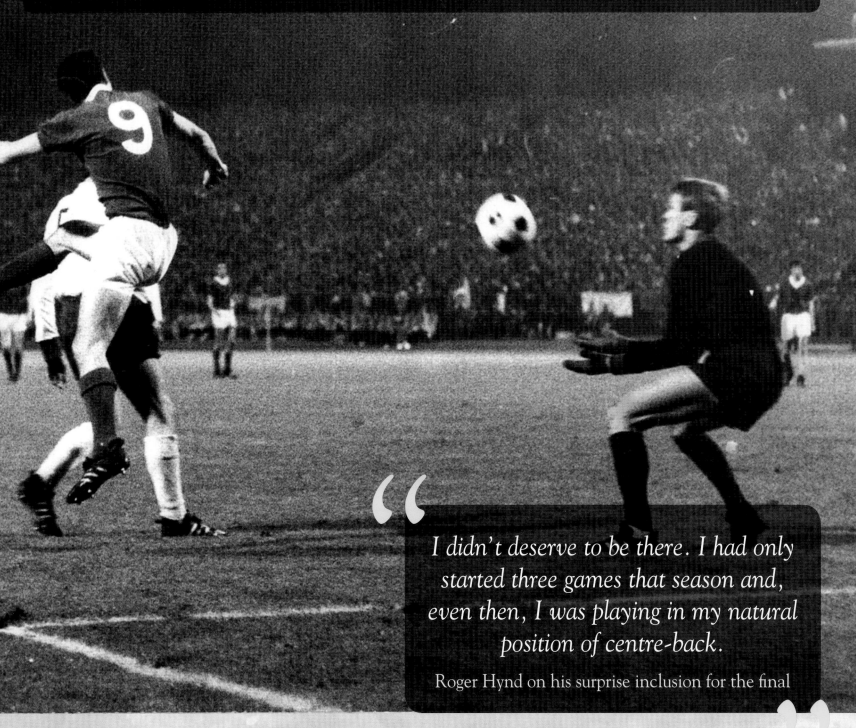

The repercussions of the shock defeat by Berwick in the Scottish Cup went far beyond Scotland. With Forrest and McLean departed, and an on-form Alec Willoughby strangely overlooked by manager Symon, centre-half Roger Hynd was played at centre-forward against Bayern, having played fewer than a handful of games all season. Although a willing workhorse, he notoriously missed a sitter when the game was goalless although he did have a "goal" controversially ruled off for a challenge on Bayern keeper Sepp Maier. Here he is having a header saved by the legendary German keeper. Franz Roth scored the crucial goal in extra time to take the cup the short distance back to Munich.

"

I didn't deserve to be there. I had only started three games that season and, even then, I was playing in my natural position of centre-back.

Roger Hynd on his surprise inclusion for the final

"

Barcelona Here We Come

Rangers would get their revenge against Bayern five years later in the semi-final of the Cup Winners' Cup. After scraping a rather fortuitous 1-1 draw in the first leg in Munich, expectant Rangers fans in a crowd of 80,000 at Ibrox wait on the arrival of the teams for the return game. On a unique night for Scottish football, at the other end of the city, Celtic fans were turning up at Parkhead for their European Cup semi-final second leg against Inter Milan. The later kick-off for that game meant that many Rangers fans were back home in time to see the Italians win through on penalties.

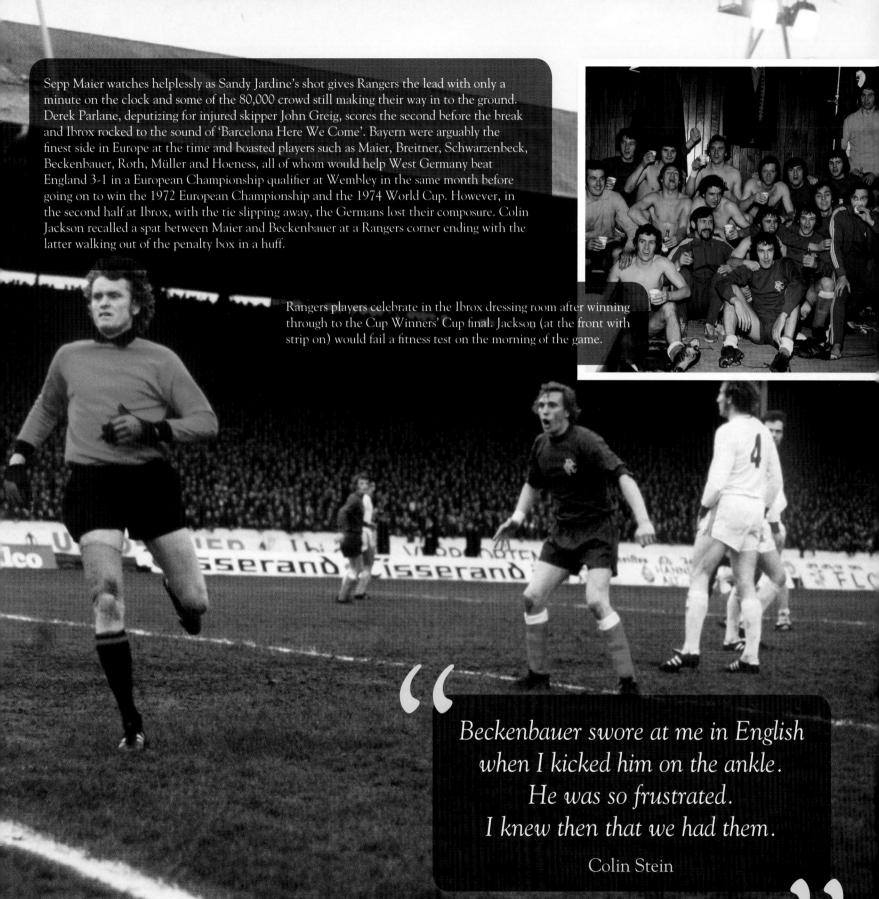

Sepp Maier watches helplessly as Sandy Jardine's shot gives Rangers the lead with only a minute on the clock and some of the 80,000 crowd still making their way in to the ground. Derek Parlane, deputizing for injured skipper John Greig, scores the second before the break and Ibrox rocked to the sound of 'Barcelona Here We Come'. Bayern were arguably the finest side in Europe at the time and boasted players such as Maier, Breitner, Schwarzenbeck, Beckenbauer, Roth, Müller and Hoeness, all of whom would help West Germany beat England 3-1 in a European Championship qualifier at Wembley in the same month before going on to win the 1972 European Championship and the 1974 World Cup. However, in the second half at Ibrox, with the tie slipping away, the Germans lost their composure. Colin Jackson recalled a spat between Maier and Beckenbauer at a Rangers corner ending with the latter walking out of the penalty box in a huff.

Rangers players celebrate in the Ibrox dressing room after winning through to the Cup Winners' Cup final. Jackson (at the front with strip on) would fail a fitness test on the morning of the game.

" *Beckenbauer swore at me in English when I kicked him on the ankle. He was so frustrated. I knew then that we had them.*

Colin Stein "

79

ABOVE: John Greig exchanges pennants with counterpart Valeri Zykov. Greig missed the second leg of the semi-final with a foot injury and was touch and go for the final.

LEFT: Rangers team line up at the Nou Camp, the night before the game. Back row, left to right: trainer Stan Anderson, coach Jock Wallace, John Greig, Derek Johnstone, Bobby Watson, Andy Penman, Alfie Conn, Willie Johnston, Graham Fyfe, Colin Jackson, Gerry Neef, Tommy McLean, Peter McCloy. Front row, left to right: Alex MacDonald, Dave Smith, Jim Denny, Colin Stein, Sandy Jardine, Alex Miller, Derek Parlane, Willie Mathieson.

> " *I knew where I was putting it, just a glance to knock it in to the corner.*
>
> Willie Johnston "

The final could hardly have started better for Rangers. Colin Stein fired the Light Blues in the lead after 24 minutes and, here, Willie Johnston scores the second five minutes before the break with a header from a Dave Smith cross as Alex MacDonald looks on.

ABOVE: Johnston celebrates his strike.

BELOW: Alex MacDonald in the thick of a Rangers attack with Derek Johnstone in support. When Willie Johnston scored his second just after the break to make it 3-0 it seemed the match was over. However, while Rangers had finished their season the Russians were still in the midst of their league campaign and were becoming fitter and fresher. They stormed back with goals from Eshtrekov and Makhovikov, and in the end the Scots were holding on desperately.

> *If the game had gone another 5 or 10 minutes, Rangers would have been caught.*
>
> Rangers fan Billy McMahon

Over-enthusiastic Rangers fans grab Greig in the post-match celebration; the Ibrox skipper grimaces as someone stands on his injured foot.

"

One of the officials handed the trophy to me with hardly a word and then we were back on our way to the dressing room. It was one of the greatest nights of my career but in the end it was a real slap in the face for Rangers.

John Greig

"

Daily Record

BARCELONA BATTLE

Rangers win Cup ..then fans riot

3p Thursday, May 25, 1972 No. 33,877

Players mobbed on the pitch

THE SHAME IN SPAIN

BARCELONA: MIDNIGHT
Alex Cameron reports

THOUSANDS of Rangers fans fought a pitched battle with baton-swinging Spanish police here last night.

It happened at the end of the most unruly major European soccer match ever.

The scene after Rangers had beaten Moscow Dynamo 3-2 in the Cup Winners' Cup final were fantastic.

It was chaos. A total shambles. A blot on sport and those who watch it.

Charged

It took Rangers players nearly 10 minutes to fight their way through the mobbing, milling thousands, who rushed on to the pitch in the worst mass invasion ever at a big game in Europe.

And it was the FIFTH time that the fans had scurried madly on to the great Barcelona pitch from their seats on the steep tiers of concrete.

Finally the pistol-packing policemen, who had shown a stoic apathy, lost their heads at the end of the match.

They charged into the ground with batons swinging madly. Fans were bludgeoned to the ground.

White-coated ambulance men rushed around to attend to fans with blood streaming from their faces.

Yelling

The police charged the unruly mob three times, baton-swinging before the windmills among the fans.

But the most astonishing scene of all was when herds of yelling fans leapt from the terracing and chased the police halfway across the pitch in disorder.

Other fans hurled

CONTINUED ON BACK PAGE

Rangers captain John Greig mobbed by wildly excited fans as they invade the pitch.

THE TENSE TRIUMPH ● **VICTORY AND VIOLENCE**

See Page 27   See Centre Pages

ABOVE: Free from the clutches of the exuberant Rangers' supporters, Greig relaxes in the bath with the trophy. Instead of clearing the pitch to allow the presentation, the Spanish militia began striking out at the fans: a battle ensued and a night of glory was tarnished. Consequently, the Ibrox skipper was presented with the cup deep in the bowels of the Nou Camp. Rangers were banned from Europe for two years, which was later reduced to one on appeal.

Returning Heroes

The next day over 20,000 fans turn up in the rain to see Rangers return to Ibrox with the European Cup Winners' Cup. The players go round the running track on the back of a hastily decorated lorry. Perhaps there were no open-topped buses available.

A pipe band leads the Rangers players around Ibrox in their victory celebration.

20,000 FANS HAIL IBROX HEROES

Daily Record

REVELS IN THE RAIN!

3p, Friday, May 26, 1972 No. 23,878

THIS was it! The moment Rangers brought the European Cup-winners' Cup home to Ibrox—with 20,000 fans revelling in the rain.

On a red, white and blue-decked lorry, captain John Greig, his team-mates clustered around him, held the Cup aloft.

And slowly, proudly, the triumphant progress began—two circuits of the stadium,

STORY BY KEN STEIN   PICTURES BY ERIC CRAIG

with cheering, cheering, all the way.

Many of the fans, just back from Barcelona, were still wearing souvenir sombreros.

They waved them and their banners and their scarves—and yelled themselves hoarse.

Before the team appeared, a loudspeaker announcement had warned that "stringent action" would be taken

against anyone who invaded the rain-soaked pitch.

But, warnings or weather, nothing could dampen the good-natured enthusiasm of the crowd.

Earlier, Glasgow's Lord Provost John Mains had met Rangers chairman John Lawrence and the team when they flew into Prestwick Airport.

But all of that was just the curtain-raiser to the fantastic welcome at the stadium.

This was an Ibrox night of nights, a time to stand up and cheer.

And they did, 20,000 of them, like cheering had just been invented.

Police said later: "There was no trouble at the ground. Only two arrests were made—outside the stadium."

Willie's hat-trick —Back Page   ●   **Follow, Follow—See Centre Pages**

–LEGENDS–

Jock Wallace

Jock Wallace was the first man to have been Rangers manager twice and, in the first stint between 1972 and 1978 he guided the Light Blues to two trebles in the space of three seasons.

Born in Wallyford, Midlothian, and a boyhood bluenose, he had been a goalkeeper with Airdrie and West Bromwich Albion and of course had played for Berwick Rangers when they had inflicted the humiliating 1-0 defeat on the Ibrox men in 1967. The Light Blues fans would forgive him, and then some.

When Waddell brought Wallace to Ibrox in 1970 both coach and players soon found out that the former Jungle fighter was a fitness fanatic, although his players maintain there was more to his football than fighting spirit.

Wallace shocked football when he resigned as Rangers boss in 1978 and journeyed south to manage Leicester City, winning them promotion to the old English First Division.

He returned to Scotland in 1982 to manage Motherwell, and when Greig stepped down as Rangers boss the following year, Wallace was invited back to the fold, although the Ibrox board had first courted Dundee United manager Jim McLean and then Aberdeen boss Alex Ferguson.

Wallace's second period was less successful, despite winning two League Cups, and he left in April 1986 to be replaced by Graeme Souness. He went on to manage Seville, in Spain, and Colchester United, but his heart belonged to Ibrox and he still holds a special place in the affections of the Rangers support.

Wallace is lifted high in the air by players at Easter Road in 1975 after Rangers clinched the First Division title to prevent Celtic making it 10 in a row. There were around 25,000 Light Blues fans in a crowd of 35,000 at the home of Hibs to see Colin Stein's header giving the visitors a point and the championship in a 1-1 draw.

FOOTBALL
–STATS–

Jock Wallace

Name: John "Jock" Wallace

Born: 1935

Died: 1996

Rangers manager: 1972–78, 83–86

Achievements: Scottish League 1975, 1976, 1978. Scottish Cup 1973, 1976, 1978. League Cup 1976, 1978.

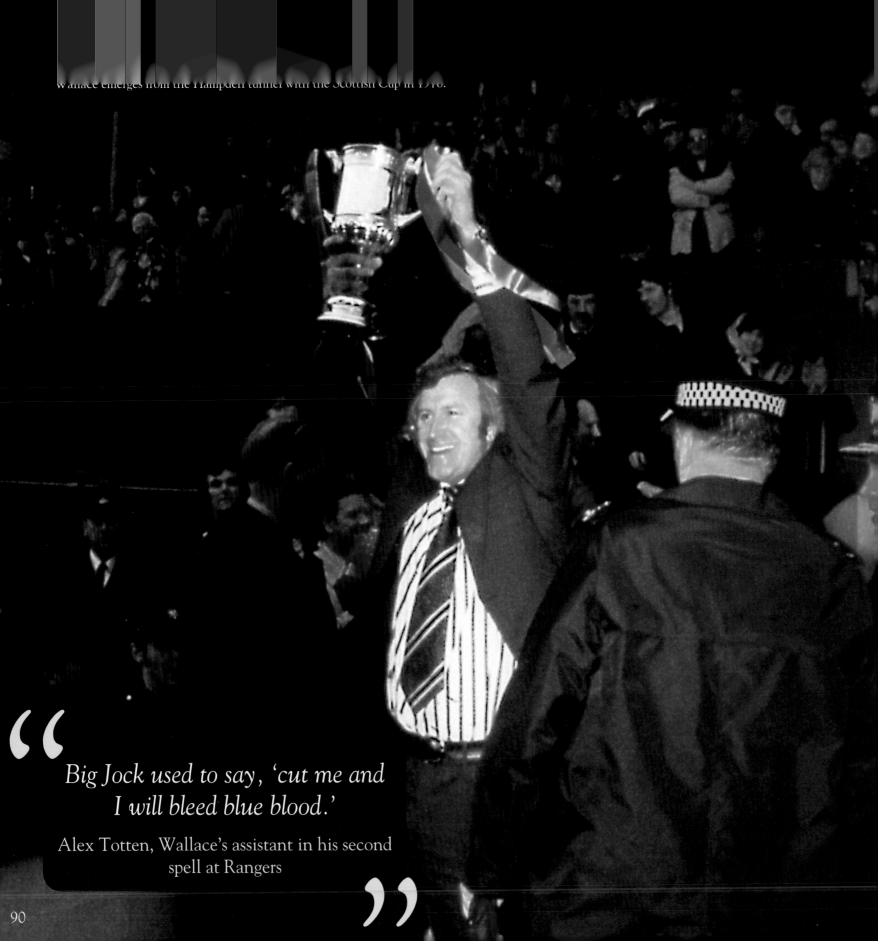

Wallace emerges from the Hampden tunnel with the Scottish Cup in 1976.

" *Big Jock used to say, 'cut me and I will bleed blue blood.'*

Alex Totten, Wallace's assistant in his second spell at Rangers "

Wallace with a collection of trophies.

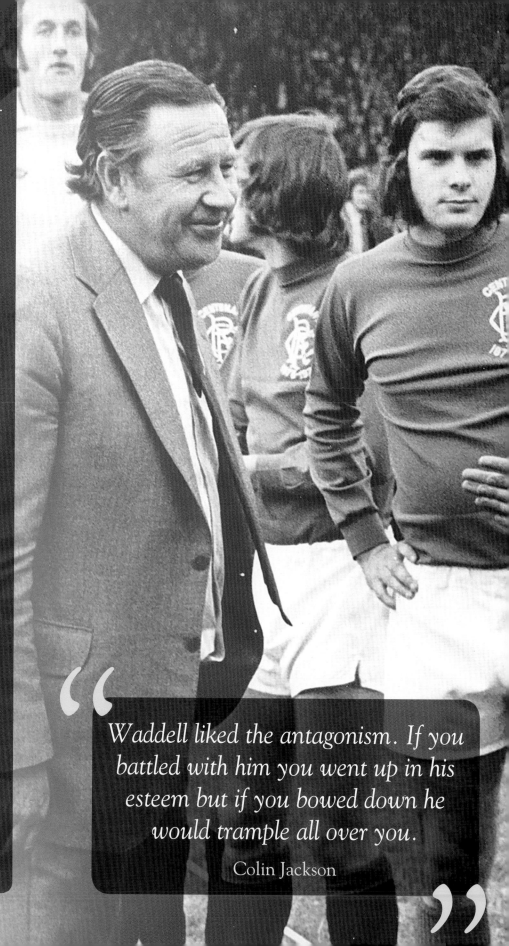

–LEGENDS–

Willie Waddell

Waddell arguably contributed more to Rangers than anyone as player, manager and executive of the club. He first played for Rangers in a reserve game at the age of 15 and was an outstanding outside-right, mostly under Struth during the late 1930s to 1950s. Indeed, "Deedle" was such a hero as a player that he had his own terracing song – 'How can you sell Willie Waddell?'

After he retired in 1956, he tried his hand at management at Kilmarnock. He succeeded in guiding them to their only Championship win in 1964–65. He subsequently entered the world of journalism but returned to Ibrox in December 1969 following the dismissal of David White. Some say Waddell's criticism of White following the European defeat by Polish side Gornik at Ibrox read like a job application. Nevertheless, he proved to be up to the job on and off the park. However, with his infamously dour and often abrasive personality Waddell was respected rather than loved. He went on to serve the club in managing director, general manager and vice chairman roles until his death in 1992. His biggest legacy is that he drove through the redevelopment of Ibrox.

RIGHT: A smiling Waddell talks to his former players Colin Stein and Willie Johnston with Derek Johnstone stripped and ready for action.

> "Waddell liked the antagonism. If you battled with him you went up in his esteem but if you bowed down he would trample all over you.
>
> Colin Jackson

FOOTBALL
-STATS-

Willie Waddell

Name: William Waddell

Born: 1921

Died: 1992

Playing career: Rangers 1938–1955

Appearances: 601

Goals: 153

Rangers manager: 1969–1972

Matches: 131

ABOVE: Waddell gives the Ibrox crowd one of his lectures during half-time in a game against St Mirren in 1978. He was occasionally scathing of the fans. In the wake of Barcelona, he was less than conciliatory when he addressed the troublesome section of the Rangers support: "It's to these tykes, hooligans, louts and drunkards that I pinpoint my message. It is because of your gutter rat behaviour that we are being publicly tarred and feathered."

The Sweet
SEVENTIES

If a picture paints a thousand words – two legends, two different characters. In 1972, following the Cup Winners' Cup final win, Willie Waddell moved upstairs at Ibrox to become general manager and Jock Wallace took over as boss. There was always talk of tensions between the two men. Wallace forever refused to reveal the reasons why he dramatically resigned in 1978 – which endeared him further to the Rangers fans – but it is thought that a falling out with Waddell over money to buy new players lay behind his shock decision. However, before that day arrived, Rangers would enjoy a fair measure of success.

1972 Rangers win the European Cup Winners' Cup by beating Dynamo Moscow 3-2 at Camp Nou in Barcelona. Within weeks, manager Willie Waddell moves to the general manager position with coach Jock Wallace appointed boss. **1973** Rangers beat Celtic 3-2 in the Scottish Cup final at Hampden watched by Princess Alexandra. **1975** A nine-year period of Celtic dominance in the league comes to an end as Rangers win the title with a 1-1 draw against Hibs at Easter Road. **1976** The Ibrox club win the domestic treble and emulate the achievement two years later. **1978** Wallace shocks Scottish football by resigning as Rangers boss and steadfastly refuses to divulge the reason for his departure. John Greig makes the step up from captain to manager. **1979** The course of Greig's managerial career takes the first wrong turning when Rangers lose the title to Celtic in a 4-2 defeat at Parkhead.

LEFT: Wallace continued with his philosophy of hard work when he became manager. Here he gives Alex O'Hara a helping hand – or foot – as he puts the players through their paces at the infamous Gullane sands on the east coast of Scotland. The Ibrox players would run up and down the dunes, one of which was called Murder Hill, until they were exhausted – then they would do it again. In the early 1970s Scottish football had yet to embrace sports science and thus throwing up was often used as guidance when assessing the effectiveness of a session.

BELOW: Rangers players at the top of the hill waiting for their turn to descend.

> *Everyone knows Jock felt pre-season training was important. I felt I could run forever.*
>
> Colin Stein

First In, Best Dressed

RIGHT: Willie Henderson finds himself "piggy in the middle" at training. Henderson left Rangers in acrimonious circumstances before the Cup Winners' Cup final, replaced on the wing by Tommy McLean, whom Waddell had signed from his former club, Kilmarnock.

BELOW: Rangers players make their way across from Ibrox to the Albion training ground. Note the ripped top worn by Derek Johnstone (second right). When Graeme Souness arrived as player-manager in 1986 he was taken aback by the state of the club's training kit. It would often be left to dry overnight and then worn again the next day, often still caked in mud.

"

At times wee Tam McLean and myself would come out of training shattered.

Alex MacDonald

"

Doug Houston skips while Alex MacDonald, Tommy McLean and Johnny Hamilton are on the weights.

Colin Stein was a Rangers hero of the late 1960s and early 1970s. An old-fashioned, rampaging centre-forward he was the first £100,000 signing between two Scottish clubs when he was transferred to Ibrox from Hibs in 1968 – and proved his worth by scoring eight goals in his first three games. Here he is playing against his old club in the 1972 Scottish Cup semi-final. The "Celtic end" of Hampden is in the background as Stein tried to force his way in to the Hibs penalty area. He left for Coventry later in the year but returned in 1975 to help Rangers win the title.

A Royal Blue Affair

The 1973 Old Firm Scottish Cup final at Hampden was played in front of 122,714 fans and attended by royalty for the first time. Princess Alexandra meets the Rangers players before the game and is pictured shaking hands with Derek Parlane who would equalize Kenny Dalglish's opener. As a classic game unfolded, Alfie Conn restored Rangers' lead a minute after the break when he stretched away from the Hoops' defence before George Connelly levelled from the spot, leaving the unlikely figure of Tom Forsyth to become the Ibrox hero with the winning goal.

It's every player's dream to score the winner in the Cup final. Tommy McLean's free-kick is met by Derek Johnstone whose header beats Celtic keeper Ally Hunter but strikes the post and rolls along the line and hits the other upright. On hand is Forsyth, who makes an ungainly stab at the ball with his studs but forces it over the line before racing away in joy. The big defender nicknamed "Jaws", like Kai Johansen in 1966, is forever to be remembered for his Scottish Cup final winner.

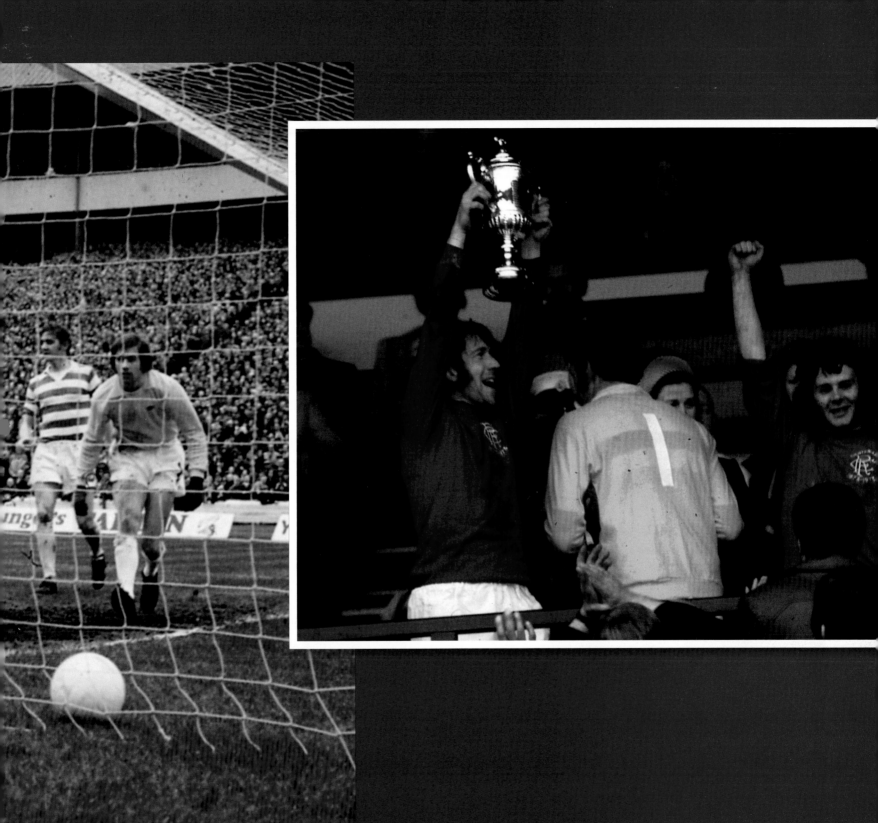

ABOVE: Greig accepts the trophy from Princess Alexandra and holds it aloft to the cheers of the Rangers supporters. Peter McCloy picks up his medal while Alfie Conn raises his fist in triumph.

The talented Alfie Conn was a favourite of the Ibrox fans before moving to Tottenham in 1974. A member of the Cup Winners' Cup team, he also scored several important goals against Celtic. However, the midfielder stunned the Light Blue faithful when he returned to Scotland in 1977 to play for the Parkhead side, thus becoming the first man in the post-war era to play for both Old Firm clubs. He played in the Celtic team that beat Rangers in the 1977 Scottish Cup final at Hampden (becoming the first man to win Scottish Cup medals with both Glasgow giants) and spent most of the match listening to scathing chants from the Rangers support. However, Conn, son of Hearts legend Alfie Conn senior, was inducted into the Rangers "Hall of Fame" in 2007, which shows a level of forgiveness at the Ibrox club – although redemption is not yet complete.

Conn models the Celtic shirt after signing for the Parkhead club.

Johnstone v Johnstone. In a League Cup section tie at Parkhead in August 1973, Celtic's Jimmy Johnstone chases the ball while his Rangers' namesake Derek looks to clear. Derek Johnstone often played at centre-back but his ability to score goals meant he spent most of his career in attack.

ABOVE: After scoring his Cup final winner in 1973 Forsyth returned
to what he did best – tackling. Here is a typically boisterous challenge
on Hearts striker Willie Gibson in a league game at Ibrox in 1975.

RIGHT: Sandy Jardine of Rangers and Kenny Dalglish of Celtic in an
Old Firm photocall in 1975, both looking rather self-conscious. For
some reason Jardine is not wearing any footwear.

BELOW: Rangers players take the acclaim of the fans after winning the league title at Easter Road in 1975.

Alex 'Doddy' MacDonald celebrates after scoring the winner against Celtic in the 1975 League Cup final at Hampden.

Alex MacDonald was always good at stealing in to the box to get on the end of things.

Sandy Jardine

RIGHT: MacDonald was a tenacious midfielder who could be relied on to come up with important goals. Here he is being held aloft by Derek Johnstone after scoring against Hearts in the 1976 Scottish Cup final at the national stadium. Rangers won 3-1 to complete the domestic treble, although the game is remembered for Johnstone scoring the opener in 45 seconds. The game had started earlier than the official 3 o'clock kick-off time, so that many fans missed the goal.

RIGHT: In the semi-finals Rangers beat Motherwell while Hearts beat Dumbarton 3-0 in a replay. The Jambos' task was made easier when a Sons player called Walter Smith scored an own goal. The future Rangers manager is seen flying through the air at Hampden to head past his helpless keeper.

It's a
Family Affair

LEFT: Alex Miller, John Greig, Stewart Kennedy, Sandy Jardine and Alex MacDonald pose proudly with their children in front of the Scottish Cup.

–LEGENDS–

Davie Cooper

Davie Cooper came to the attention of Rangers fans in 1976 when he gave the Ibrox side a hard time playing for Second Division Clydebank in a League Cup quarter-final tie in which it took two replays before the Light Blues went through. In the first game in Govan, Cooper scored the match-saving equalizer in a 3-3 draw.

The Hamilton-born winger was signed in 1977 by Jock Wallace for £100,000 and over the next decade and more he would become a hero. Amid regular moments of magic he scored unforgettable goals against Celtic in the 1979 Drybrough Cup final and Aberdeen in the 1987 League Cup final. Although, like most wingers, he was prone to inconsistency, at his best he toyed with defenders and was peerless with a dead ball. He won 24 caps for Scotland (20 of them with Rangers) and played in the World Cup in Mexico in 1986.

He moved to Motherwell in August 1989 for £50,000 and helped the Fir Park club to win the 1991 Scottish Cup, defeating Dundee United 4-3 in a memorable Hampden final. On 22nd March 1995, at the age of 39, he collapsed and died of a brain haemorrhage the following day. Scotland was stunned.

Cooper flanked by Tom Forsyth and John Greig, who has his training top embroidered with MBE in recognition of the honour he was awarded in 1977.

" I played for the team I loved.

Davie Cooper

LEFT: Cooper in Clydebank colours goes past John Greig, who would become his future team-mate and manager. It was no secret that both men did not see eye to eye and Cooper was somewhat stagnating during Greig's tenure as boss until Graeme Souness arrived to rejuvenate the winger.

FOOTBALL
–STATS–

Davie Cooper

Name: Davie Cooper

Born: 1956

Died: 1995

Playing career: Rangers 1977–1989

Appearances: 540

Goals: 75

The public display of affection and respect at Ibrox following Cooper's death.

–LEGENDS–

John Greig

In 1999 John Greig was voted by Light Blues fans as the "Greatest Ever Ranger", an accolade with which few would disagree.

He made his debut against Airdrie in 1961 and went on to have a glittering career which saw him play in three treble-winning sides (1964, 1976 and 1978). He played mostly as a defensive wing-half and latterly as a defender. In total he won five league titles, six Scottish Cup winners' medals and four League Cup medals – and, of course, captained the club to the European Cup Winners' Cup triumph in 1972. The boyhood Hearts fan also skippered Scotland and won 44 caps.

However, arguably, it was his spirit and determination to keep fighting during Celtic's nine-in-a-row years that elevated him to the highest level in the minds of the Rangers fans. Greig, like the Gers support, endured the Hoops' dominance in the decade that spanned the 1960s and 1970s with a stoicism that made subsequent success all the sweeter.

He moved from the dressing room to the hot seat the day after Jock Wallace quit in 1978. His time as boss was less successful, although it has to be said he suffered some bad luck. In his first season Rangers won the League Cup and Scottish Cup but were pipped for the title by Celtic. Despite further cup success, the championship was to elude him and he left in 1983. Greig returned in 1990 in a PR role, and in early 2004 he became a director of the club.

"
Greigy was Rangers – he epitomised the club and still does to this day.

Derek Johnstone

"

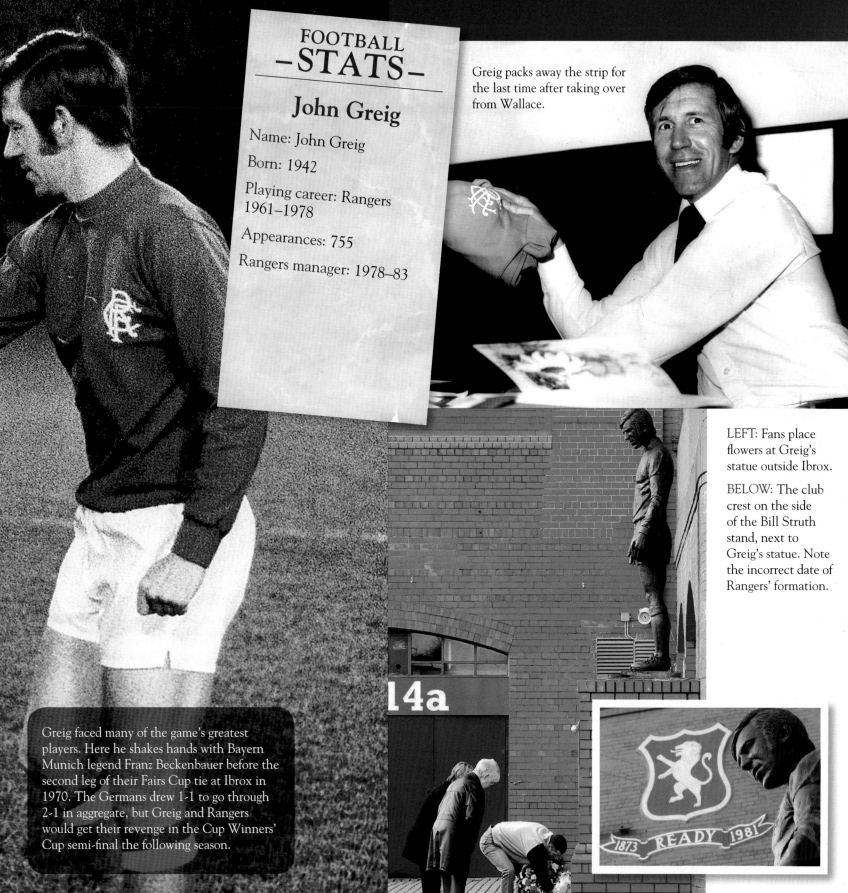

FOOTBALL
–STATS–

John Greig

Name: John Greig

Born: 1942

Playing career: Rangers 1961–1978

Appearances: 755

Rangers manager: 1978–83

Greig packs away the strip for the last time after taking over from Wallace.

LEFT: Fans place flowers at Greig's statue outside Ibrox.

BELOW: The club crest on the side of the Bill Struth stand, next to Greig's statue. Note the incorrect date of Rangers' formation.

Greig faced many of the game's greatest players. Here he shakes hands with Bayern Munich legend Franz Beckenbauer before the second leg of their Fairs Cup tie at Ibrox in 1970. The Germans drew 1-1 to go through 2-1 in aggregate, but Greig and Rangers would get their revenge in the Cup Winners' Cup semi-final the following season.

14a

1873 READY 1981

Who's that with John Greig?

No Rod Stewart interview is complete without reference to his love for Celtic, but here the legendary singer is resplendent in the 1977 Rangers strip along with Greig.

ABOVE: A musical role for Greig as he tries his hand with a set of bagpipes.

LEFT: A man alone. Greig is only in the manager's job three months and finds he is already distanced from his former team-mates. Pictured sitting at the front of the new film centre at Inverclyde in Largs.

Gordon Smith (future SFA chief executive) fires in a shot under pressure from Aberdeen defender Willie Miller in the 1979 League Cup final at Hampden. Goals from Alex MacDonald and Colin Jackson took the cup back to Ibrox. Rangers also won the Scottish Cup that season but lost the title to Celtic when they went down 4-2 at Parkhead.

MacDonald opens the scoring for Rangers in their "title decider" at Celtic Park but it was ultimately to no avail as the home side, reduced to 10 men early in the second half, battled back. The match is remembered incorrectly as the last game of the season, but in fact Rangers had still to play Partick and Hibs and thus only Celtic could have won the championship that night.

Ibrox is in the midst of redevelopment as it hosts a typically frenetic Old Firm game. Celtic skipper Roy Aitken crunches Ally Dawson in their first meeting of the 1979/80 season, which ended in a 2-2 draw.

1980 Cup Final Riot and Other
TROUBLES

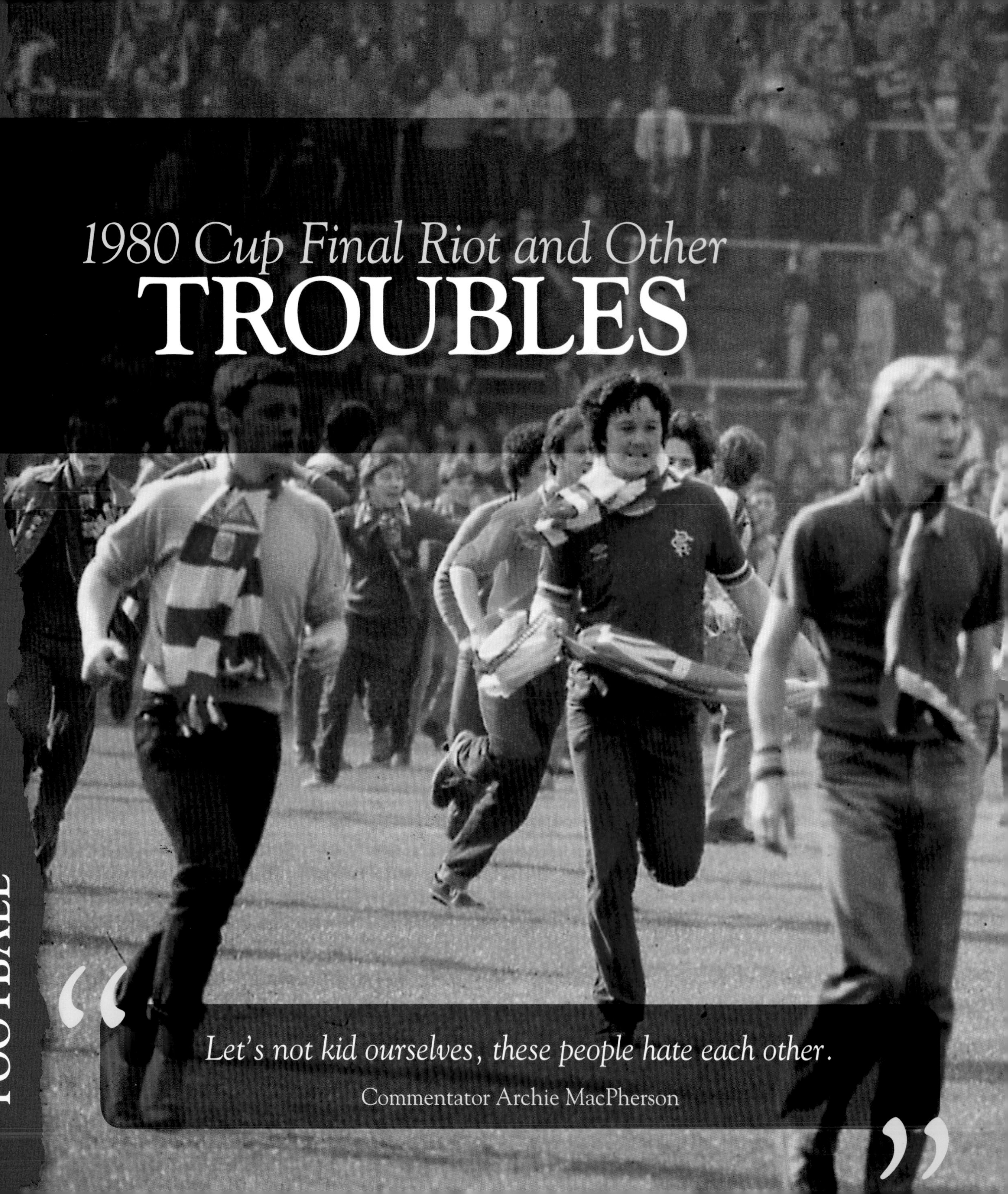

"

Let's not kid ourselves, these people hate each other.

Commentator Archie MacPherson

"

At the end of the 1909 Old Firm Scottish Cup final replay at Hampden, which ended in another draw, supporters of Rangers and Celtic joined forces to riot, feeling they had been fleeced by the authorities, who had requested another replay. At the end of the 1980 Old Firm Scottish Cup final at the same venue, following a 1-0 extra-time win for Celtic, the fans fought each other. Times had changed. In the intervening years the rivalry between the two clubs had moved from sporting to mostly sectarian. Celtic were still closely associated with their Irish Catholic roots while Rangers had taken on the mantle of the Protestant alternative. There had been various skirmishes at Old Firm games in previous decades but the pitched battle on the hallowed Hampden turf was witnessed by a worldwide audience and was discussed in the House of Commons and the House of Lords. The riot hastened the introduction of legislation that banned alcohol at sporting arenas in Scotland, with the Ibrox club taking most of the blame for their 'no-Catholic' signing policy. Like most clubs, Rangers had intermittent hooligan problems at home, with incidents in away-games dating back at least to the 1960s at Wolverhampton and Newcastle through to Barcelona, Manchester and Birmingham in the 1970s.

Charge towards the Celtic end.

Rangers supporters on the Hampden pitch.

With most of the police outside the stadium waiting for the fans to come out, some minutes elapsed before order was restored. The sight of police on horseback charging up and down the pitch trying to force fans back over the fences remains the burning memory for many people, while 22-year-old WPC Elaine Mudie, on a white horse called Ballantrae, enjoyed 15 minutes of fame in the aftermath.

1980 was a low point for Old Firm relations, but the Sixties and Seventies were also a dark time for Rangers as far as hooliganism was concerned. This did not always involve rival fans, however: it was not uncommon to see gang fighting on the terraces behind the goal at Ibrox during games. The League Cup section game against Celtic at Ibrox in August 1973, which the visitors won 2-1, was disrupted by crowd trouble.

Police tangle with Gers supporters behind the goal.

Alfie Conn watches as police race to try and stem the pitch invasion.

Police move through the Rangers fans on the terracing.

127

1969 Scottish Cup final. Hundreds of Rangers fans spill on to the park after Stevie Chalmers scores Celtic's fourth goal in the 4-0 win.

ABOVE: Rangers keeper Stewart Kennedy runs to the dressing room as mayhem ensues at Villa Park. The "friendly" game in October 1976 was abandoned early in the second half, with the visitors losing 2-0. There were numerous arrests, mostly of Scottish fans.

1980s: *Lowest Low to*
HIGHEST HIGH

Colin Jackson sinks to his knees in relief after Ian Redford scores a dramatic injury-time equalizer against St Johnstone in the Scottish Cup at Muirton Park in February 1981. To the left, Saints' young protégé Ally McCoist is stunned by the goal which gives the visitors a 3-3 draw. McCoist would go to Sunderland before he arrived at Ibrox in 1983, where, after a tricky start, he would become a Light Blues legend. Rangers beat the Perth men 3-1 in the replay (with McCoist scoring for the visitors) and went on to reach the final where they met Dundee United – but on that occasion Redford was the villain.

Dundee United keeper Hamish McAlpine saves Redford's last-minute penalty in the 1981 Scottish Cup final which ended goalless. A virtuoso display by Davie Cooper in the replay helped Rangers to a 4-1 win.

1980 Old Firm fans riot after Celtic win the 1980 Scottish Cup final. 1981 Rangers win the Scottish Cup with a replay win over Dundee United. 1983 John Greig signs Ally McCoist from Sunderland then later resigns as manager as another league season unravels. Jock Wallace returns from Leicester to become boss for the second time. 1984 McCoist scores a hat-trick as Rangers beat Celtic 3-2 in the League Cup final. 1986 Wallace sacked after Rangers had dropped to fifth place in the league. Graeme Souness is appointed as Rangers' first player-manager and wins his first trophy in October with a 2-1 win over Celtic in the League Cup final at Hampden. 1987 Rangers win the league with a 1-1 draw at Aberdeen. 1988 Souness's friend, businessman David Murray, takes over the Ibrox club. 1989 Maurice Johnston becomes first high-profile Catholic in decades to sign for Rangers.

LEFT: The night of Colin Jackson's testimonial game against Everton in November 1981.

Left to right: Gregor Steven, Aberdeen midfielder and future Celtic manager Gordon Strachan, Jackson, Celtic winger Davie Provan and Sandy Jardine. At the back is Alex Miller, Jim Stewart and Bobby Russell.

BELOW: Rangers captains through the years gather for a picture in October 1983.

Left to right: Bobby Shearer, Jock 'Tiger' Shaw, George Young, John Greig and Ian McColl.

137

The Souness Revolution

In April 1986, Graeme Souness arrived from Sampdoria to take over from Jock Wallace as player-manager of Rangers. Scottish football would never be the same again. Souness brought with him a reputation as a world-class midfielder who had enjoyed great success at Liverpool and his arrival signalled a sea-change in attitudes in Govan, a return to the days when only the best would do. Edinburgh-born Souness was a Scotland international who had simply not been on the radar at Ibrox during the previous years; but with money made available, there were more big names to come, further facilitated by Scottish businessman David Murray, who took over the club in November 1988. Souness took advantage of an open cheque book and English teams being banned from Europe at the time to attract players such as Terry Butcher, Chris Woods, Graham Roberts, Trevor Steven and Trevor Francis, among many others. He also took great delight in persuading Mo Johnston not to return to his boyhood heroes Celtic, but instead, to become the first high-profile Catholic in decades to play for Rangers.

Souness sits in frustration at Celtic Park
after Rangers go close to scoring.

Rangers midfielder Ian Durrant has the young brother of team-mate Derek Ferguson on his shoulders. Barry Ferguson would go on to captain Rangers and Scotland.

Souness made his mark immediately as Rangers beat Celtic 2-1 in the 1986 League Cup final at Hampden. This time it's Durrant who is on the shoulders of Terry Butcher as the Ibrox players celebrate.

After the game, Souness talks with disappointed Celtic players, but Mark McGhee, Murdo MacLeod and Roy Aitken don't seem interested.

Colin West, Chris Woods, Terry Butcher, Graham Roberts and Neil Woods decked out in kilts.

The best of British was the motto under Souness and here you see the club's international players in their respective strips. The Scotland players in the back row are Ally McCoist, Derek Ferguson, Ian Durrant, Robert Fleck and Davie Cooper. Northern Ireland's Jimmy Nicholl is flanked by Englishmen Terry Butcher and Chris Woods.

The Title Returns

LEFT: May 1987. At the end of Souness's first full season Rangers travelled to Pittodrie in the penultimate game of the season, needing a point to clinch the title. There were Light Blues fans in all four sides of the ground and hundreds outside when Terry Butcher headed the opener. Ally McCoist jumps on his back with Dave MacPherson coming in to join the celebration. In typically controversial fashion Souness was sent off, but the game ended 1-1 and the first championship in nine years was at Ibrox.

ABOVE: Butcher gets carried away in the post-match Pittodrie celebrations.

A shirtless Graham Roberts tries to escape down the tunnel at Pittodrie after Rangers clinch the title. Thousands of visiting fans had invaded the pitch, and with shades of Wembley 1977, the cross bar was snapped. The Ibrox club immediately promised to pay for the damages.

Police guard the goal but the damage is done.

Old Firm Madness

Souness began his tenure at Ibrox playing down the intensity of the Old Firm. He said he would not mind if Celtic beat Rangers four times in the season so long as his team ended up with the title, but he soon got caught up in the madness of it all. In the first Glasgow derby of the 1987/8 season he picked up yet another red card, this time for a foul on Hoops' midfielder Billy Stark as Rangers went down 1-0 at Parkhead. But in terms of Old Firm mania, there was worse to come at the next meeting at Ibrox.

Goldilocks and the Three Bears

Celtic's visit to Ibrox in October 1987 ended in a 2-2 draw but resulted in three Rangers players and a Parkhead player appearing in court. The game went down as one of the most infamous in Old Firm history and one of the most dramatic in Ibrox folklore. With the game goalless, Celtic striker Frank McAvennie clashed with Ibrox keeper Chris Woods, and, after skipper Terry Butcher intervened, McAvennie ended up on the ground. When calm was momentarily restored, McAvennie and Woods were sent off and Butcher was booked. With no substitute keeper, Graham Roberts took over in goal and before the interval Celtic were 2-0 up. Andy Walker gave the visitors the lead before Butcher scored an own goal. In the second half Butcher got involved with Celtic keeper Alan McKnight and he too was sent packing after picking up a second yellow card. It looked a lost cause for the Light Blues, but McCoist pulled a goal back for the nine-man home side and Richard Gough scrambled in a last-minute equalizer. Roberts conducting a sing-song moments later (for which he was charged by the police) while in possession of the ball remains an iconic image. The aftermath saw a highly publicized court case involving McAvennie, Butcher, Woods and Roberts, who were nicknamed Goldilocks and the Three Bears. All four were charged with behaviour likely to cause breach of the peace. Butcher and Woods were found guilty and fined £250 and £500 respectively, while Roberts and McAvennie were cleared.

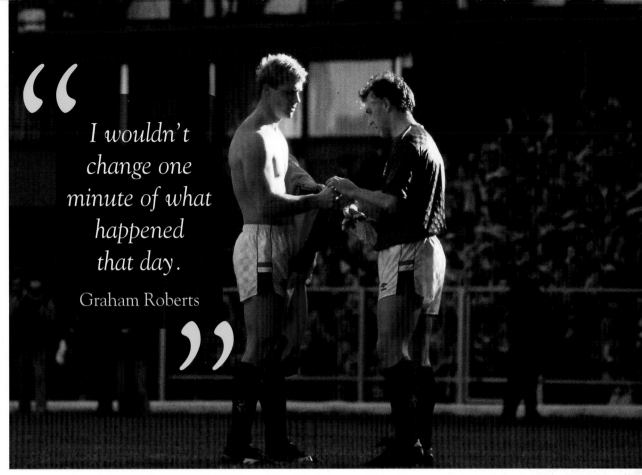

> " *I wouldn't change one minute of what happened that day.* "
>
> Graham Roberts

ABOVE: Woods gives Roberts the goalkeeper's jersey before he departs.

BELOW: Woods gets first use of the home dressing room showers.

There are Rangers fans who claim they have never heard such a noise at Ibrox as when Gough forced in the dramatic late equalizer against Celtic.

ABOVE: The Rangers players arrive at court with club officials and legal representatives. The case turned in to something of a circus.

Walters' Woes

When he joined the club from Aston Villa on New Year's Eve 1987, Mark Walters became the first black player to play for Rangers. He made his debut on 2nd January 1988 in the Old Firm derby defeat by Celtic at Parkhead. The Englishman was on the end of some vicious racial abuse from the "Jungle" section of Parkhead, with bananas being thrown on to the trackside. This was almost totally ignored by the media and Walters became a firm favourite of the Ibrox support during his three and a half years at the club. H is now an honorary member of the Rangers Supporters Trust.

Mark Walters runs out for his Parkhead debut.

LEFT: No Englishman at Ibrox was free from the threat of being pictured in a kilt.

Once a Ranger, Always a Ranger

"Once a Ranger, always a Ranger" is an old Scottish football maxim. Jock Wallace was just one of many Rangers fans at Brockville for the last game of the 1987/8 season. He watches his former team win 5-0, but the Light Blues finished third that season behind Celtic and Hearts.

Arguably the most infamous tackle in the history of Scottish football was witnessed at the Aberdeen versus Rangers game at Pittodrie on 8th October 1988. Captured in all its gory detail is Neil Simpson's appalling challenge on Ian Durrant, which sidelined the young Rangers mdifielder for 30 months with knee ligament damage. A huge crowd turned up at Ibrox in April 1991 to see his return in a reserve fixture against Hibernian, and he eventually forced his way back into the successful Rangers side of the early 1990s, although many believe he never reached his previous heights. After a loan spell at Everton he moved on to Kilmarnock for four years. The Simpson incident added to the enmity that has grown between Aberdeen and Rangers over the last 20 years.

> "One minute you're the brightest star since the one over Bethlehem, the next it's all taken away from you."
>
> Ian Durrant

Durrant recuperating at home.

159

A Nettle Grasped

All Scotsmen know where they were on 10th May 1989, when hearing that Maurice Johnston had signed for Rangers (the author was on holiday in Greece). One newspaper could not wait to see the former Celtic striker paraded in blue for the first time, so it mocked up this picture of him in a Rangers shirt. The Ibrox club had operated a "no Catholics" policy for decades and there were plenty of doubters when Graeme Souness said he would sign players regardless of race, creed or colour. It emerged in later years that several Catholics had turned him down before the phlegmatic Johnston took the plunge. He had played for the Hoops, his boyhood heroes, between 1984 and 1987 before moving to Nantes in France. He returned two years later and weeks before signing for Rangers he appeared at a press conference at Celtic Park where he declared that "Celtic are the only club that I want to play for". No contracts were signed at that point, however, and so, in a remarkable act of one-upmanship, Souness persuaded him to go across the city to Ibrox. The details of the deal are still shrouded in mystery, but the significance was crystal clear.

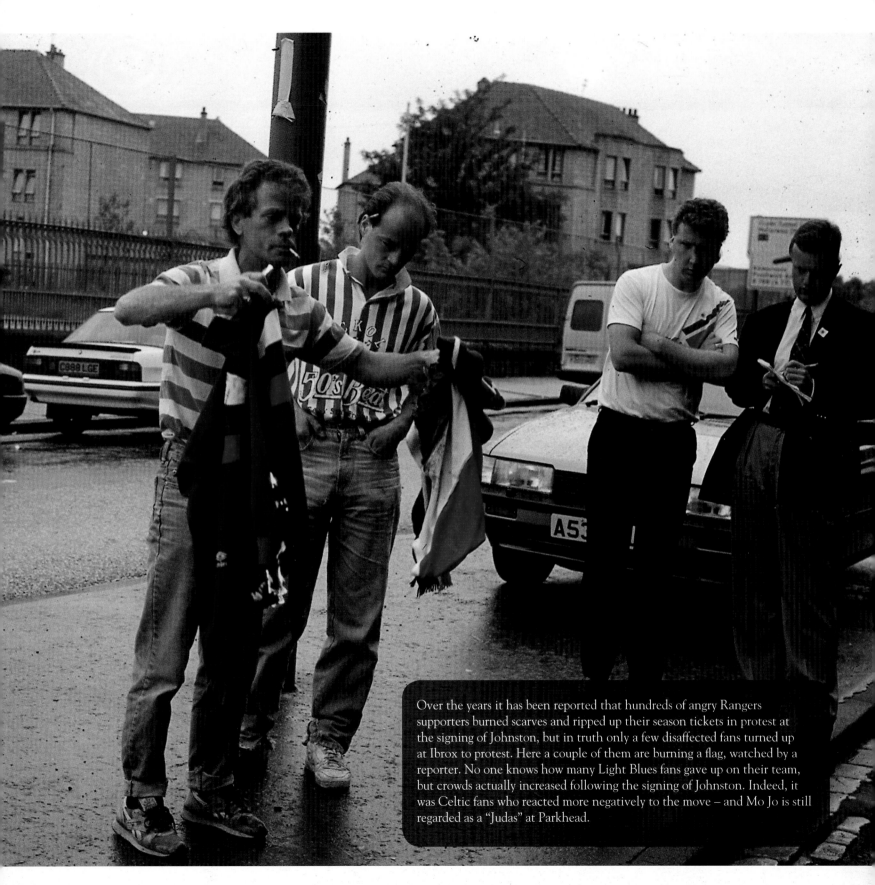

Over the years it has been reported that hundreds of angry Rangers supporters burned scarves and ripped up their season tickets in protest at the signing of Johnston, but in truth only a few disaffected fans turned up at Ibrox to protest. Here a couple of them are burning a flag, watched by a reporter. No one knows how many Light Blues fans gave up on their team, but crowds actually increased following the signing of Johnston. Indeed, it was Celtic fans who reacted more negatively to the move – and Mo Jo is still regarded as a "Judas" at Parkhead.

Johnston was understandably given a hard time by Celtic fans in August 1989 when he trotted out at Parkhead in blue for a game that ended 1-1.

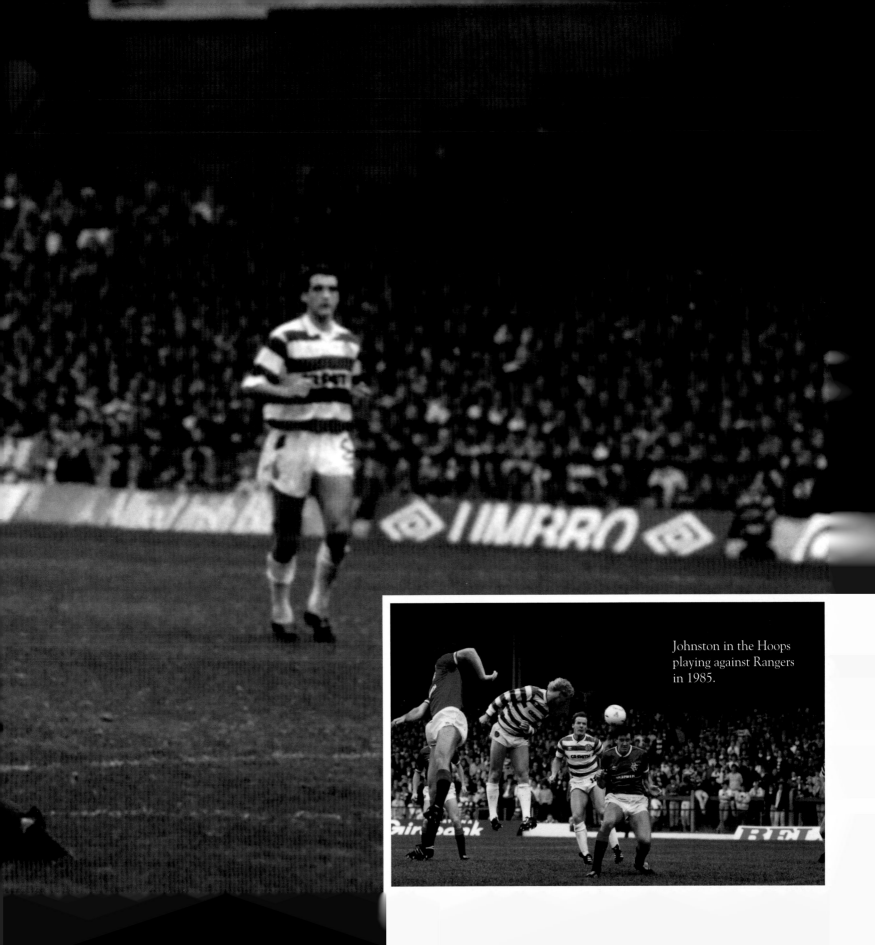

Johnston in the Hoops
playing against Rangers
in 1985.

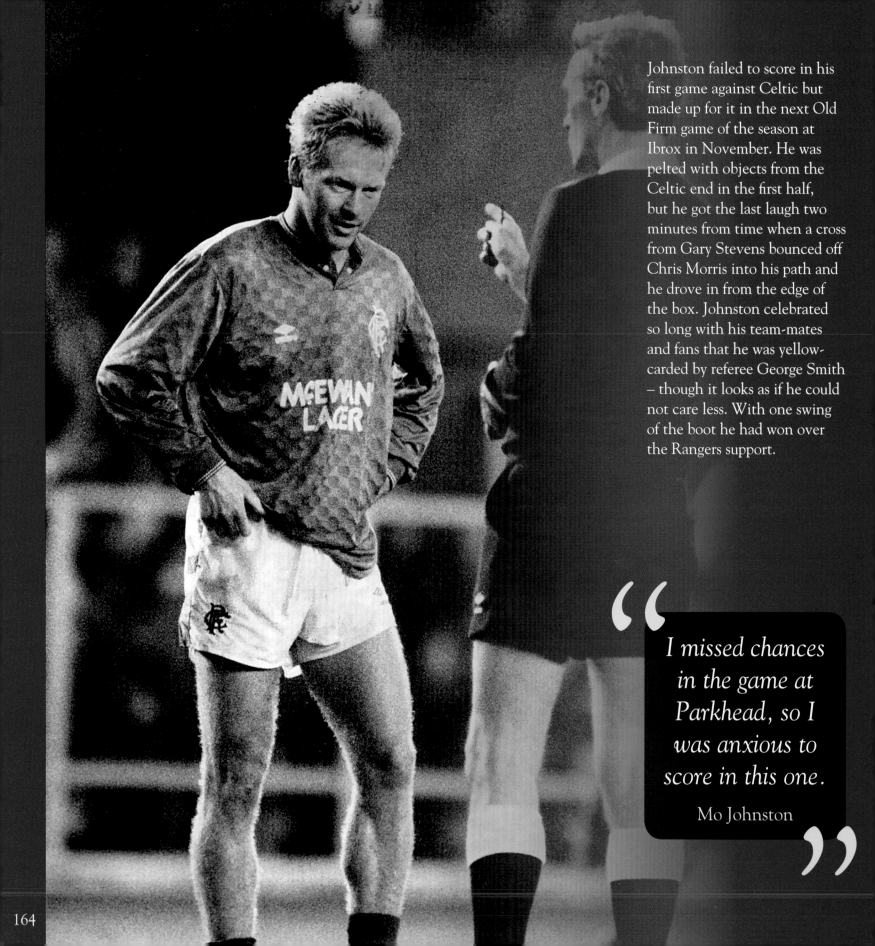

Johnston failed to score in his first game against Celtic but made up for it in the next Old Firm game of the season at Ibrox in November. He was pelted with objects from the Celtic end in the first half, but he got the last laugh two minutes from time when a cross from Gary Stevens bounced off Chris Morris into his path and he drove in from the edge of the box. Johnston celebrated so long with his team-mates and fans that he was yellow-carded by referee George Smith – though it looks as if he could not care less. With one swing of the boot he had won over the Rangers support.

> " *I missed chances in the game at Parkhead, so I was anxious to score in this one.* "
>
> Mo Johnston

Johnston celebrates with Walter Smith.

The Changing Face of
IBROX

Ibrox stadium is one of Scotland's most famous landmarks and one of Europe's better football arenas. Its majestic red-bricked Main Stand, now named the Bill Struth Stand, is designated as a Category B listed building and the stadium has been awarded five star status by UEFA.

Rangers played their first games at Flesher's Haugh at the Glasgow Green. The first ground of its own was at Burnbank, in Glasgow, which opened in 1875, before the club moved to Kinning Park the following year. Next came a move to Ibrox, just west of Kinning Park, for the start of the 1887/8 season. The Light Blues soon outgrew that ground and in 1899, under the guidance of Scottish engineer and Rangers fan Archibald Leitch, built another one (practically on the same site) where they have stayed ever since.

The stadium has gone through radical changes over the years, some of which were enforced. In 1902 Ibrox hosted the Scotland versus England international where 25 people were killed and 517 injured when part of the wooden west terracing collapsed. It was football's worst disaster at that time.

Remedial improvements improved safety and comfort and increased capacity, but the next major development was in 1929 with the completion of the new 10,500-seater Main Stand, designed by Leitch, who was responsible for designing stands at many other grounds, such as those for Arsenal, Celtic, Manchester United, Everton, Tottenham Hotspur, Chelsea and Aston Villa. Over 118,000 packed in to the stadium in January 1939 for the Old Firm derby against Celtic. This remains the record attendance for a league match in Britain. Subsequent developments included a cover for the east terrace, the "Rangers end".

Two years after the second Ibrox disaster in 1971 the popular north terrace was filled with benches and renamed the Centenary Stand (note that the club were still going with the formation date of 1873 at that time), but this was no more than a temporary measure until the stadium was redeveloped in a more radical way.

The Copland Road Stand (colloquially known as the Rangers end) was completed in 1979 and originally accommodated 7,500 spectators (later increased to around 8,000). An identical stand (the Broomloan Road Stand) was completed in 1980 at the opposite end.

In 1981, the bigger Govan Stand, accommodating 11,000 spectators, was completed. The stands had turned Ibrox from a bowl shape into a box, but in the mid-1990s the three new stands were linked and the corners filled with seats with screens situated above.

The Main Stand was altered in 1991 to include another tier (the club deck) and the last standing areas of the stadium, the east and west enclosures at the front of the stand, were seated. The capacity is currently around 52,000. The Main Stand was renamed the Bill Struth Main Stand in September 2006 to commemorate the 50th anniversary of the death of the club's most celebrated manager.

LEFT: Ibrox Stadium.

BELOW: Leitch's Main Stand as it used to look.

> "Rangers' Main Stand is Leitch's 'greatest work'… still resplendent today in its red brick glory under a modern mantle of glass and steel."
>
> Simon Inglis, noted expert on football stadia

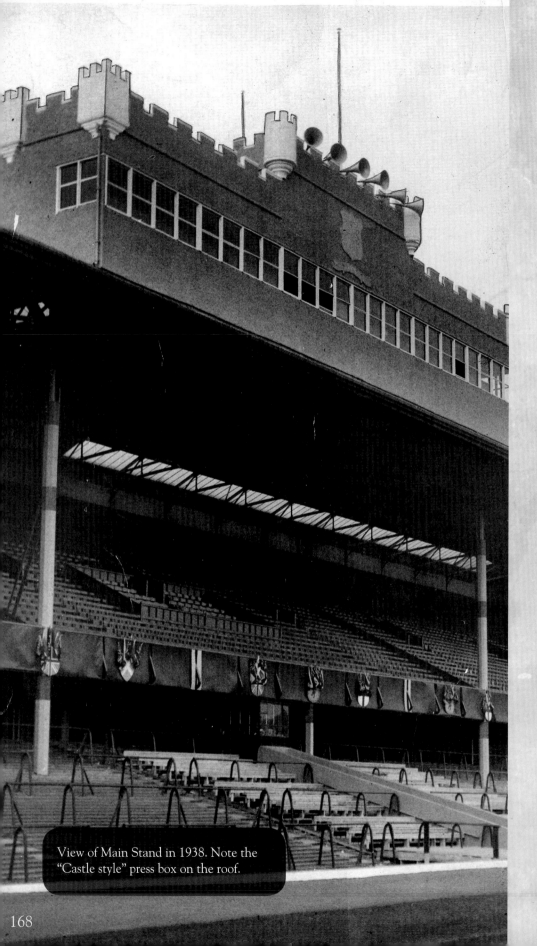

View of Main Stand in 1938. Note the "Castle style" press box on the roof.

Aerial views of Ibrox, two with the stadium empty and one with a large crowd watching a game. The exact dates are unknown but before the mid-Sixties.

"It's the home of famous heroes
And their praises have been sung –
Willie Waddell, Torry Gillick
Alan Morton and George Young.
So when all my life has ended
And when death has made its mark,
May you scatter all my ashes
On the slopes of Ibrox Park."

Verse from a traditional Rangers song

Ibrox was also famous for its sports days, which were important elements of the sporting calendar until they ended in 1962. Ian Dunbar, a Glasgow University student from Stranraer, second from left, wins the 100 metres invitation at the Glasgow Sports Day in June 1955. Less than 10 minutes after this picture was taken he was on his way to Westerlands to run for Glasgow in the Scottish inter-university championships where he finished second. He was keeping good company. Eric Liddell, the Scottish 400 metres Olympic champion from the 1924 Games in Paris, whose story was depicted in the Oscar- winning film *Chariots of Fire*, trained for a time at Ibrox.

Ibrox in the early 1970s. A roof had been added to the east terracing ("the Rangers end"). At that point you could still change ends at half-time.

LEFT: March 1979 and a snowbound Ibrox means the European Cup second-leg tie against Cologne has been postponed, but the new Copland Road stand takes shape.

BELOW: The massive girder for the Main Stand is lifted into place. The new seated area would be called the Club Deck.

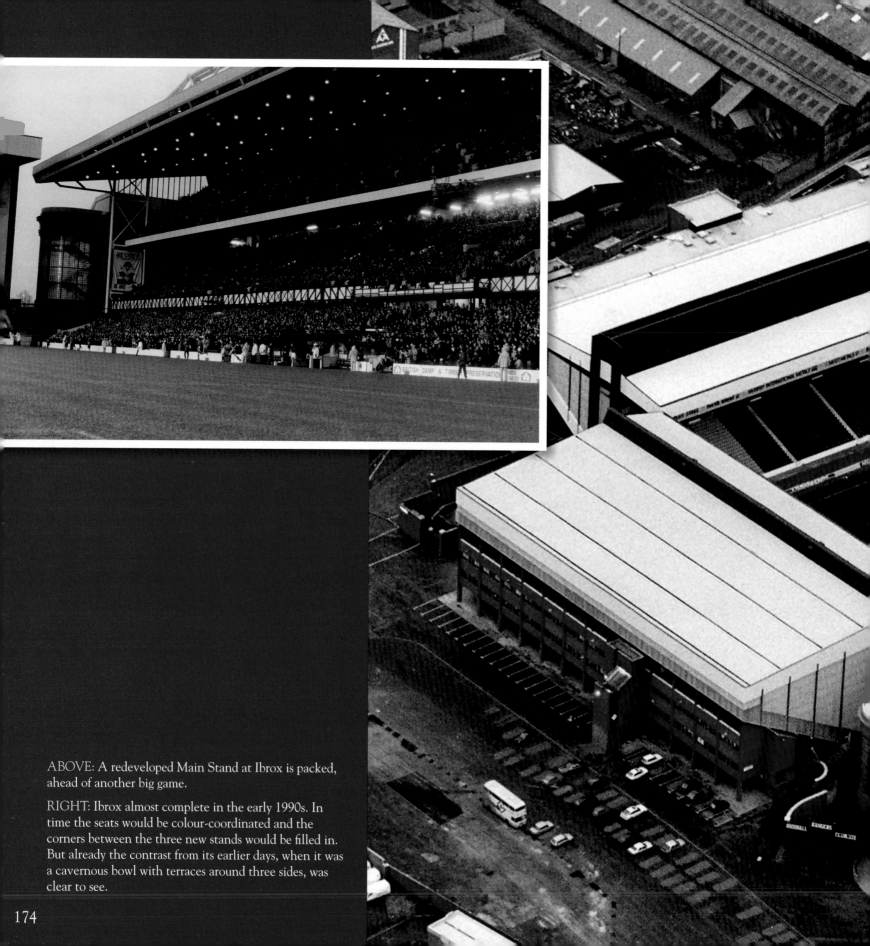

ABOVE: A redeveloped Main Stand at Ibrox is packed, ahead of another big game.

RIGHT: Ibrox almost complete in the early 1990s. In time the seats would be colour-coordinated and the corners between the three new stands would be filled in. But already the contrast from its earlier days, when it was a cavernous bowl with terraces around three sides, was clear to see.

Smith Emerges from the
SHADOWS

The 1990s and Rangers fans enjoy another good day at Ibrox. Under the calm and measured guidance of former assistant boss Walter Smith, who had taken over from Souness in 1991, the Govan club moved inexorably towards nine titles in a row, matching Celtic's similar achievement in the mid-1960s to mid-1970s. However, while there was plenty of domestic success for Gers fans to gorge upon, Europe proved more frustrating.

1991 Souness leaves for Liverpool, replaced by his assistant, Walter Smith, who steers the side to a last-day title-winning victory over Aberdeen at Ibrox. **1993** Rangers win the domestic treble and come within one match of reaching the Champions League final. **1994** Rangers win the double but miss out on a back-to-back domestic treble after losing in the Scottish Cup final to Dundee United at Hampden. **1995** England star Paul Gascoigne causes great excitement when he signs from Lazio. **1996** The Light Blues hammer Hearts 5-1 in the Scottish Cup final, with Gordon Durie scoring a hat-trick. **1997** Rangers win their ninth championship in a row, thereby equalling Celtic's achievement. **1998** Smith leaves Ibrox at the end of a barren season and Rangers appoint their first foreign manager, Dick Advocaat. It is the end of an era.

Scottish football was undergoing radical changes on and off the park in the early Nineties, but the Old Firm tensions remained stable. Rangers increased their stranglehold on the Scottish game, racking up titles and trophies. The treble was won in 1992/3 and the Light Blues came within a game of reaching the final of the newly revamped Champions League. Celtic fans, of course, were less than enamoured. Here one tries to attack Rangers keeper Ally Maxwell at Parkhead, but he had not reckoned on John "Bomber" Brown, who deals out his own justice before stewards and police arrive on the scene.

Insurrection in front of the director's box at Celtic Park. Hoops supporters fight among themselves as their team is on its way to another defeat by Rangers. Amid it all sits Walter Smith, trying to look inconspicuous. Rangers directors, including Donald Findlay and Campbell Ogilvie, sit to Smith's right, while David Murray and John Greig are in the row behind.

–LEGENDS–

Ally McCoist

Ally McCoist remembers well when, during a poor performance against Dundee at Ibrox in his early days, most of the Copland Road stand joined in a chorus of "Ally, Ally, get to f***." It was his darkest day in Light Blue but not only did he go on to win the fans over, he became a hero whose charisma and personality transcended Ibrox and, indeed, Scottish football. "Super Ally" holds the Rangers record for league and European goals and he was the club's leading scorer in 9 of his 15 seasons. His highest total in the league was 34, which he reached three times in 1986/7, 1991/2 and 1992/3.

McCoist regularly terrorized Celtic, which added to his hero status. He is second in the list of Rangers scorers in Old Firm games with a total of 27.

His last goal for Rangers came in his last match in Light Blue, the 1998 Scottish Cup final defeat by Hearts. McCoist, who scored 19 goals for Scotland and played in the 1990 World Cup in Italy, left to join Kilmarnock where he played for three years before retiring. He was awarded an MBE in 1994 for his services to Scottish football.

Playing to the gallery as usual. To the delight of the photographers, McCoist takes a call on a mobile phone (when they were still relatively new) following title-winning celebrations at Ibrox in 1992.

FOOTBALL -STATS-

Ally McCoist

Name: Alistair Murdoch McCoist

Born: 1962

Playing career: Rangers 1983–1998

Appearances: 581

Goals: 355

Who's that with Ally?

> *Every supporter of every club likes Ally.*
>
> Former Scotland boss Craig Brown

McCoist chats with former Prime Minister Margaret Thatcher. Helped by an appearance on the television programme *Question of Sport*, Ally became well known all over Britain.

McCoist teams up with Muhammad Ali.

McCoist with Joe Strummer of The Clash at Scotland's biggest musical festival, T in the Park, August 1995.

A satisfied McCoist is substituted after scoring a hat-trick against Alania Vladikavkaz in the Champions League qualifier. Rangers won 7-2 in Russia to go through 10-3 on aggregate.

Let Me
Entertain You

RIGHT: Pop superstar Robbie Williams wears his
Rangers shirt under his jacket on his way to the Old Firm
game in August 1994.

LEFT: The European Cup Winners' Cup squad of 1972 get together 25 years later for a reunion. Back row, left to right: Craig (physiotherapist), Neef, Miller, Parlane, Denny, Johnston.

Middle, left to right: Johnstone, Jackson, Conn, Mathieson, McCloy, Stein, Smith, Henderson (although he was away from Rangers by the time of the final). Front, left to right: Fyfe, MacDonald, Greig, Jardine, Anderson (coach).

ULTI METALS   NSS NORTHERN SURPL

1995 and Rangers close in on nine-in-a-row when they beat Hibs 3-1 at Ibrox to clinch number seven. Walter Smith and his players take a bow on the pitch.

-LEGENDS-

Brian Laudrup

Laudrup was destined to be a footballer. His father, Finn, was a Danish international and his elder brother Michael was a world-class player at clubs such as Juventus, Barcelona and Real Madrid.

Brian was part of the Denmark side that won the 1992 European Championships against the odds, but he arrived at Ibrox in July 1994 after an unhappy time in Italy with Fiorentina, which included a loan spell at AC Milan. However, by the end of the season he had captivated the Gers support, his trickery, vision and inventiveness helping the Light Blues to their seventh consecutive title. At times he was miles ahead of anyone in the Scottish game, with many believing they were watching the best player to wear a Rangers jersey.

Laudrup was also named Player of the Year, both by the Scottish Football Writers Association and his peers in the Professional Footballers' Association. He teamed up with Paul Gascoigne to propel Rangers to championship number eight, but arguably his finest hour was in the 1996 Scottish Cup final. Gordon Durie helped himself to a hat-trick in the 5-1 win over Hearts but was overshadowed by a mesmeric Laudrup who, apart from making all three of Durie's goals, scored two himself. However, his most famous moment came in 1997 when his header from a Charlie Miller cross against Dundee United at Tannadice clinched the record-equalling title number nine.

Laudrup takes the acclaim of the Rangers support after scoring against Celtic in the 1996 Scottish Cup semi-final at Hampden.

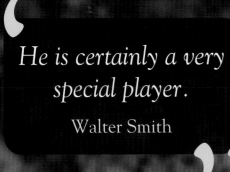

> *He is certainly a very special player.*
>
> Walter Smith

FOOTBALL –STATS–

Brian Laudrup

Name: Brian Laudrup

Born: 1969

Playing career: Rangers 1994–1998

Appearances: 150

Goals: 45

BELOW: Durie accepts the congratulations of his team-mates including Davie Robertson, John Brown and Paul Gascoigne after scoring in the 1996 Scottish Cup final against Hearts. Provider Laudrup is in a peculiar position as he crawls over to the Gers striker.

–LEGENDS–

Andy Goram

There were few dissenters in 2001 when Andy Goram was voted the greatest Rangers goalkeeper of all time. The Bury-born keeper was a mainstay of the Light Blues team, helping the Ibrox club to nine-in-a-row (he was in goal for the last six championship years) and to boot his performances against Old Firm rivals Celtic were often brilliant. Goram was not the tallest or the most athletic of footballers but his positioning was immense and his shot-stopping second to none. By the time he had left Ibrox he was simply called "the Goalie".

Goram joined Oldham Athletic as a teenager and stayed there seven years, winning the first of his 43 caps for Scotland before moving north to Hibs. While at Easter Road he became a double international when he represented Scotland at cricket.

When Walter Smith brought the keeper to Ibrox in June 1991 as a successor to Chris Woods it was perhaps the best £1 million he had ever spent. Goram had many brilliant games for Rangers but perhaps the second leg of the Champions League qualifier against Leeds United at Elland Road was the best of them all, as Rangers won 2-1 to go through 4-2 on aggregate.

Latterly troubled with knee injuries, he won three Scottish Cups and three League Cups to add to his six titles before leaving at the end of the 1998 season. It is testament to Goram that he is still known as "the Goalie".

Goram with an over-sized Rangers strip hanging off the Main Stand.

> *On my gravestone it will read Andy Goram broke my heart.*
>
> The late former Celtic boss Tommy Burns

–LEGENDS–

Richard Gough

Richard Gough led Rangers to nine successive championships during the Eighties and Nineties. The Ibrox captain was one of only three players to appear in all nine campaigns – Ally McCoist and Ian Ferguson were the others. Gough was a determined defender, good in the air at either end but it was his inspirational leadership qualities that shone as he drove Rangers and Scotland through their tougher times.

"King Richard", as he would become known to the Light Blues supporters, was a proud Scot although he was born in Stockholm and brought up in South Africa. He had a trial at Ibrox as a youngster but failed to impress and subsequently signed for Dundee United, with whom he won a SPL title medal in 1993. After a spell as skipper at Tottenham, Graeme Souness brought him to Ibrox in 1987. He was the club's first million pound signing (costing £1.1 million) and he replaced Terry Butcher as captain three years later. Gough was missing through injury when Brian Laudrup scored the goal at Tannadice that clinched the ninth successive title. He was clearly overcome with emotion as he went on to the pitch to receive the trophy in what he believed would be his last act as a Rangers player before leaving for America. However, by October 1997 he was back and played in 24 league games in his final season. He returned to America to play for San Jose Clash, but in March 1999 agreed to join English Premier League strugglers Nottingham Forest in their fight against relegation and then moved to Everton, where he played until he was 40. But "King Richard" remains forever linked to Ibrox.

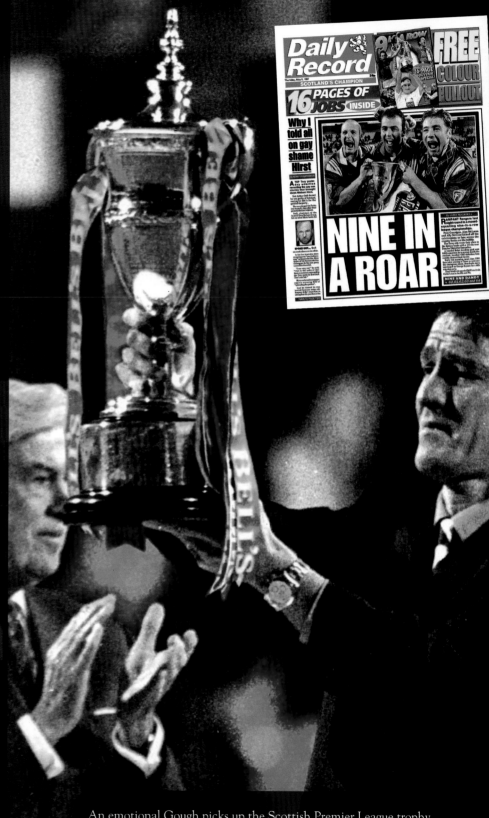

An emotional Gough picks up the Scottish Premier League trophy, the club's ninth in succession.

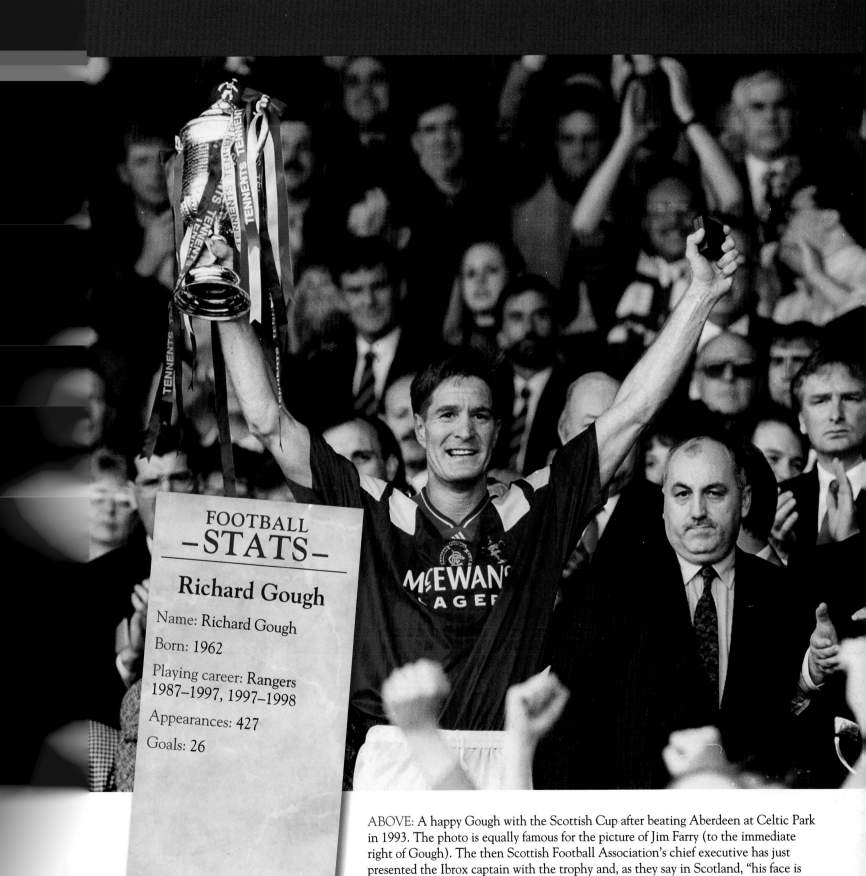

FOOTBALL
–STATS–

Richard Gough

Name: Richard Gough

Born: 1962

Playing career: Rangers
1987–1997, 1997–1998

Appearances: 427

Goals: 26

ABOVE: A happy Gough with the Scottish Cup after beating Aberdeen at Celtic Park in 1993. The photo is equally famous for the picture of Jim Farry (to the immediate right of Gough). The then Scottish Football Association's chief executive has just presented the Ibrox captain with the trophy and, as they say in Scotland, "his face is tripping him".

At Work and Play

LEFT: Rangers team outside the Kings Theatre in Glasgow to publicize Jonathan Watson's play about the club called *Follow Follow*.

At the back, left to right: Neil Murray, Peter Huistra, Ally Maxwell, Ian McCall, Ian Ferguson, Davie MacPherson, Gordon Durie, Archie Knox (assistant manager), Ian Durrant, Ally McCoist, John Brown. Front, left to right: Richard Gough, Watson, Trevor Steven.

BELOW: Rangers squad go for a run. Team spirit played a crucial part in the club's success in those days, with Richard Gough famously claiming that their mantra was "The team that drinks together, wins together."

Gazza

Paul Gascoigne's football career and indeed, his life, has routinely lurched from the sublime to the ridiculous and it's safe to say his spell at Rangers from 1995 to 1998 was no different. When the England midfielder arrived in Glasgow from Lazio there was a rush of excitement among Light Blues fans, the likes of which had never been witnessed before. From the moment he came out of the main doors at Ibrox to meet the fans who had turned up to see him following his signing, Gascoigne was a hero, as much as he had been at Newcastle, Tottenham, Lazio and for England. Problems with discipline and injuries, which had bedeviled his career hitherto, remained during his spell in Glasgow. However, those character defects could not hide the sheer talent of one of British football's greatest midfielders. While some claimed he was past his best, others thought that Scottish football was not exacting enough for his talents. Nonetheless, the genial Geordie thrilled Rangers supporters with his displays, which exuded panache and power, Glasgow "gallussness" and goals. Perhaps the highlight of his time at Ibrox was his championship-winning performance against Aberdeen at Ibrox in April 1996 when he scored a hat-trick in a 3-1 win over the Dons, who had shocked the home side by taking the lead. He left the club in March 1998 to sign for Middlesbrough, and his problems on and off the field continued. But there will always be a smile when the name "Gazza" is mentioned among Gers fans.

Gazza was taunted by opposition fans about his weight since his early days with home-town team Newcastle. Here he self-mocks with a "big belly" gesture.

Gazza with floppy Rangers hat following the 1996 Scottish Cup win over Hearts at Hampden.

Hammer of the Celts

Gascoigne explodes with joy after scoring against Celtic in a 2-0 win at Ibrox in 1996.

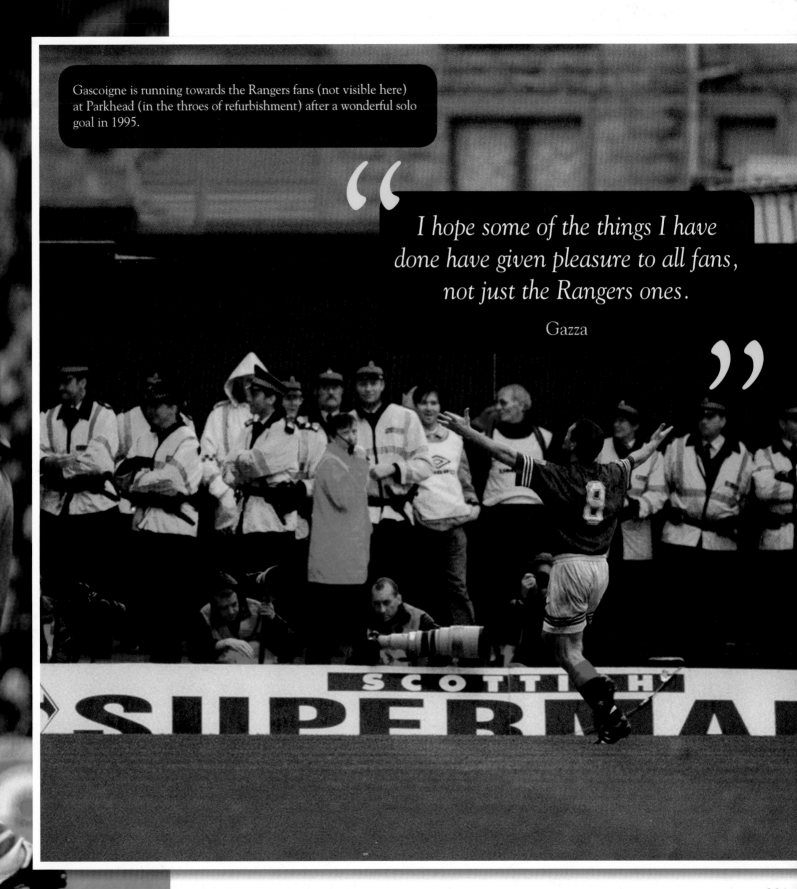

Gascoigne is running towards the Rangers fans (not visible here) at Parkhead (in the throes of refurbishment) after a wonderful solo goal in 1995.

"

I hope some of the things I have done have given pleasure to all fans, not just the Rangers ones.

Gazza

"

Sean Connery and David Murray in the director's box at Ibrox. Murray enjoyed the increase in profile which came with being the Rangers owner.

Rangers' Scottish Cup fourth-round tie against Motherwell at Fir Park in February 1998 ended in a 2-2 draw with the Ibrox club winning the replay 3-0 on the way to the final. The foundations of that cup run were not built on this defensive wall as Rino Gattuso, Alec Clelland, Marco Negri and Paul Gascoigne react none too bravely to a free-kick.

Tribute to
a Legend

LEFT: Fans lay a tribute at the gates of
Ibrox for Jock Wallace, who died in
July, 1996.

The Party's Over

Rangers finished the 1998 season empty-handed. After losing 1-0 to Kilmarnock at Ibrox, which ended SPL hopes, a distraught Gattuso, with Sergio Porrini in the background, is comforted by Andy Goram, who was out through injury. Latterly played as a full-back at Ibrox, Gattuso would move back into midfield and twice become a Champions League winner with AC Milan and a World Cup winner with Italy.

> "The bad news for Scottish football is this is as bad as it gets for Glasgow Rangers.
>
> Walter Smith

ABOVE: Walter Smith and assistant Archie Knox sit in the Celtic Park stand after the 2-1 defeat by Hearts in the 1998 Scottish Cup final. Smith had revealed he would be leaving the club in the summer earlier in the season, which many believe led to the Govan club missing out on a 10th successive SPL title. Rangers fans looked forward to Dutch coach Dick Advocaat arriving in the summer as Rangers sought to go on to the "next level". It was assumed that the Ibrox club had seen the last of Smith...

Advocaat leaves Ibrox after a visit earlier in the 1997/8 season to formulate his takeover plans.

For Kirsty, Alex and Mhairi; my team.

This book would not have been possible without the help and patience of Ann Marie Nimmo and Brian Gallagher from the *Daily Record* picture library. Thank you.

Thanks also to my old pal Adam Powley and Paul Moreton, Richard Havers, Kevin Gardner, Becky Ellis and David Scripps for help and guidance.

Graham Walker, Robert McElroy and George Wells are acknowledged experts on Rangers and offered invaluable help while agent Mark Stanton continues to steer a steady course when I'm often thinking of jumping overboard.

Last but not least, thanks to the generations of photographers who have helped capture the vagaries of the game we love.